# HAMAD BIN ABDULAZIZ AL-KAWARI

# THE
# GLOBAL
# MAJLIS

## AN INTELLECTUAL AUTOBIOGRAPHY

Translated by Karim Traboulsi

دار جامعة حمد بن خليفة للنشر

HAMAD BIN KHALIFA UNIVERSITY PRESS

Hamad bin Khalifa University Press
P O Box 5825
Doha, Qatar

www.books.hbkupress.com

ISBN: HB: 9789927118784

2  4  6  8  10  9  7  5  3  1

Typeset by York Publishing Solutions, Noida, India
Printed and bound in Great Britain by
CPI Group (UK) Ltd., Croydon CR0 4YY

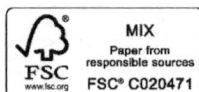

To find out more about our authors and books visit www.books.hbkupress.com
Here you will find extracts, author interviews, details of forthcoming events and the
option to sign up for our newsletters.

# Contents

# Foreword

*Resolutions are as good*
*As the resolute; generosity*
*As the generous*
*Trivial men exaggerate*
*Trivial matters*
*Great matters are overcome*
*Without effort by the great.*

*− Abu al-Tayeb al-Mutannabi*

I have written this book in stages and chapters that imposed themselves on me insistently whenever I recalled a memory or an event. In the beginning, the material consisted mainly of my comments on Instagram and texts I wrote on my mobile phone. But as the material gradually coalesced to express a certain vision and reflect a set of opinions, I decided to piece them all together into a book, to highlight the link between those scattered events and observations, bonding them with my views on issues such as culture, diplomacy, heritage, art and literature.

It is for this reason that I considered these chapters an 'intellectual biography'. It was not my original intention to write an autobiography, a form that has certain requirements and which would be premature for me to write. But the connections that emerged among the observations, remarks and short texts I was posting on social media prompted me to take a closer look and reorder them in a way that would make their reading a smoother and more coherent process.

The chapters of this book may be read separately, as each addresses a specific issue in as complete a manner as possible. They are also part of a connected and progressive narrative, representing a unified intellectual vision that is the essence of my knowledge, positions and opinions on life, culture, diplomacy and related topics.

In these pages I tackle the issue of distinctive cultural character versus universal cultural character in the context of culture and development. I describe how my perception of literature and the arts has evolved. I talk about the public space as a place for public discussion, beginning with the *majlis* tradition in our countries and extending to new media trends.

I also shed light on some of the basic aspects of cultural diplomacy, its nuances, mechanisms and objectives. In another chapter, I deal with the issue of dialogue between cultures as a way to build understanding between people and as a path to peace. I particularly focus on the cultural foundations of multilateral negotiations.

I dedicate an entire chapter to education, the 'royal road' to freedom, expressing my opinions on this cornerstone of human development. I could not omit my views regarding the link between culture and industry, through new concepts prevailing in our world today in creative and cultural industries.

The world we live in is full of instances of extremism and criminality disguised in religious garb. With this in mind, I dedicate a chapter to the crimes perpetrated against humanity and human heritage, with particular focus on Mali, Syria and Iraq.

The reader will discover, by linking the chapters together, that my perceptions are the result of the responsibilities I shouldered, as much as from the fact that I was keen for culture and its broader implications to act as a guiding light for my work. As a young man, I was appointed ambassador to serve in many countries. After working in Beirut and Damascus, I represented my country in Europe; my residence was in Paris but I was in charge of Qatar's diplomatic missions in other European countries as well. I moved later to the Americas, serving as ambassador in Washington and as ambassador extraordinary to several South American nations.

As fate would have it, part of my diplomatic mission would be ultimately devoted to multilateral action, whether as Qatar's envoy to UNESCO or as permanent representative to the United Nations in New York.

My political contributions were inseparable from my interest in culture and cultural issues. Ultimately, culture became my main preoccupation, when I was appointed first minister of culture and information from 1992 to 1997, and then minister of culture, arts and heritage from 2008 to the present day.

In this book I do not intend to recount personal experiences for the purpose of storytelling. I want to present the fruit of decades of experience in taking on cultural, educational, media and diplomatic issues. I see it as both a duty and a pleasure to share my experiences, in the hope that this will open new horizons, impart fresh ideas and broaden the space for debate and intellectual exchange.

The book is also an invitation to the reader to ponder the future of culture in our country and beyond, in the extensive world of people and intellect.

*Hamad bin Abdulaziz Al-Kawari*

# Introduction
# The Sea and the Desert: Cultural Bearings

One of the most beautiful verses of poetry that I, like most Arab school children, memorised as a child, was uttered by Al–Mutannabi, a genius of Arabic poetry and language. He wrote:

> *Man can never gain everything he hopes for*
> *The winds blow against what ships desire.*

But the truth is that I do not agree with the great poet here. I believe that it is possible to attain one's goals, if the will is there and the factors conducive to success are secured and achieved. My poetic response to Al–Mutannabi's verse would go something like this:

> *The winds blow as our ships go*
> *We are the wind, the sea, the ships*
> *He who diligently seeks shall gain*
> *What he hopes for against the odds*
> *So seek the highest goals boldly*
> *The winds always favour resolve.*

I retain these verses in the recesses of my memory and they surface often as I sit in my home opposite the sea in Ras Laffan in northern Qatar, contemplating the charm and majesty of the sea, the vast desert stretching behind me. There, on the azure horizon, I can often see giant LNG tankers emerging out of Ras Laffan heading to all corners of the earth. This is a sign of the success of Qatar in the region and the world, which would not have been possible but for the will to work and the determination to succeed.

Sitting there watching the sea and recalling Al-Mutannabi's verses, my thoughts intermix with images and scenes forming in my mind. An unconscious stream of memories plays out in succession, like a well-made film, together with profound emotions not unlike those of a person who 'has left nature itself confused', as another great Arab poet, Al-Maari, once said, or like a person with an unbearable lightness of being, to borrow from Milan Kundera.

Between those old verses, which form part of my culture and literary tastes, and modern prose, through to modern cinema, there are many eloquent ways to capture the experiences we live in today's world. Fierce winds are blowing from all directions – the winds of conflict, poverty, disease and ignorance – clashing with the winds of astounding progress in technology and culture. The more steps humanity makes towards freedom and progress, the more we see it, paradoxically, retreating, sometimes in the direction of primeval forms of oppression and backwardness.

I grew up in a culture where a celebrated caliph once said, 'If an animal should stumble on a road in Iraq, then God may hold me accountable and say, "Why did you not pave the road for it, Omar?"' The responsibility Omar speaks of here may not be actual and direct, but, rather, a moral responsibility arising from a cultural fabric woven with noble values and principles, whose ultimate goal is the happiness and well-being of all sentient creatures.

I have always believed that the compass in my mind and in the minds of all leaders points clearly towards the direction we must take and the goals we must pursue, despite adverse winds and currents.

The metaphor of the ship rocked by sea winds is not random, occurring to me only because I am overlooking the sea. The tale of Noah and the flood is present in all monotheistic faiths, and in the myths and legends of many cultures. Its significance and implications are shared across many civilisations, although the details of the various versions differ.

The ship, or more aptly the ark, was built to save the righteous from the deluge that flooded everything, to preserve the seed of life from the devastation. On the ark pairs of all living beings, humans and animals, tame and wild, set their conflicts aside and come together peacefully against the overwhelming threat. This motif recurs frequently, reaffirming humanity's desire to live together in peace.

It is easy to find in the metaphors of the ark and the flood some expression of the current state of our world. Today, there is a deluge of ideas, perceptions, feats and cultures, carrying with it, as a sweeping tide would, a jumble of contradictory and often selfish interests, tendencies towards domination, oppression and humiliation, along with the detritus of disease, deprivation and violence. Nevertheless, we are all on board the same ark, which has room for everyone, an ark constructed of a mosaic of cultures, races, religions and, of course, shared aspirations.

Unlike in the *Epic of Gilgamesh*, we need not send birds to learn whether the water has receded from the land. Modern humanity is now able, thanks to astounding cumulative efforts made down the centuries, to predict accurately adverse weather and take the necessary precautions. Humanity, now more than ever in control of nature, is better able to steer the ark to safety.

Meanwhile, the compass fashioned by philosophy and religion, and by the work of intellectuals of all backgrounds and attitudes, has given us a precise direction and coordinates. So what is preventing us from saving the ship despite all the signs of an impending storm and an approaching flood?

History shows that all the monotheistic faiths emerged in the vicinity of a desert. This is not surprising; deserts are often synonymous with silence, solitude and mindfulness. Before their infinite vastness, man and woman feel small and insignificant, but are also motivated to strive more and to find meaning and purpose.

I would say the desert is a giant mirror in which a person can see his or her soul and actions, through a process of introspection and self-probing that has been known at least since the time of the ancient Greek philosophers. The Greeks had a great metaphor to explain this crucial process in the life of every man and woman: to be standing on a balcony and see one's self walking underneath it.

A question begs itself here: why has humanity not embarked on collective introspection? Should this not be a mission for the nations that lead the world and their intellectual and cultural elites? If humanity is navigating a desert or a vast, turbulent sea, should there be any doubt that the best course of action would be to do so collectively, in a caravan, so to speak? Those who otherwise travel in the desert or sail alone might quickly perish. The wolves prefer to eat the outlying sheep in a flock, as the Prophet Muhammad is thought to have said, the wolf here being thirst and hunger, and war, disease, poverty and ignorance.

The sea and the desert in the Arab Gulf symbolise our past and present. The sea was once the source of our livelihoods. Our ancestors sailed over its waves to fish and trade, and dived to its floor to extract its precious pearls. The desert and its oases, meanwhile, were our home and shelter against all odds, and an inspiration for our poetry and prose.

In the present, fate has ordained that the sea and the desert should become the source of our natural wealth that has helped make the region an example of comprehensive, integrated development.

But braving the sea and the desert was rarely easy, and our ancestors suffered many difficulties and ordeals, though this did not diminish their love and awe for the ocean and the dunes.

> *They appeared as if in a dream at the top of the dune, half-hidden in the cloud of sand rising from their steps. Slowly, they made their way down into the valley, following the almost invisible trail. At the head of the caravan were the men, wrapped in their woollen cloaks, their faces masked by the blue veil. Two or three dromedaries walked with them, followed by the goats and*

*sheep that the young boys prodded onward. The women brought up the rear.*
*They were bulky shapes, lumbering under heavy cloaks, and the skin of their*
*arms and foreheads looked even darker in the indigo cloth.*

This is how Jean-Marie Le Clézio, winner of the Nobel Prize in
Literature in 2008, marvellously describes a convoy traversing the
desert, in his epic book *Désert* (1980).

*They walked noiselessly in the sand, slowly, not watching where they were*
*going. The wind blew relentlessly, the desert wind, hot in the daytime, cold at*
*night. The sand swirled about them, between the legs of the camels, lashing*
*the faces of the women, who pulled the blue veils down over their eyes. The*
*young children ran about, the babies cried, rolled up in the blue cloth on*
*their mothers' backs. The camels growled, sneezed. No one knew where the*
*caravan was going.*

*The sun was still high in the stark sky, sounds and smells were swept*
*away on the wind. Sweat trickled slowly down the faces of the travellers; the*
*dark skin on their cheeks, on their arms and legs was tinted with indigo. The*
*blue tattoos on the women's foreheads looked like shiny little beetles. Their*
*black eyes, like drops of molten metal, hardly seeing the immense stretch of*
*sand, searched for signs of the trail in the rolling dunes.*

*There was nothing else on earth, nothing, no one. They were born of the*
*desert, they could follow no other path. They said nothing. Wanted nothing.*
*The wind swept over them, through them, as if there were no one on the*
*dunes. They had been walking since the very crack of dawn without stop-*
*ping, thirst and weariness hung over them like a lead weight. Their cracked*
*lips and tongues were hard and leathery. Hunger gnawed their insides. They*
*couldn't have spoken. They had been as mute as the desert for so long, filled*
*with the light of the sun burning down in the middle of the empty sky, and*
*frozen with the night and its still stars.*

*They continued to make their slow way down the slope toward the valley*
*bottom, zigzagging when loose sand shifted out from under their feet. The*
*men chose where their feet would come down without looking. It was as if*
*they were walking along invisible trails leading them out to* ...[1]

Leading them out where? Where is humanity heading, if we assume
we are those travellers in the caravan? Towards extinction by means

of weapons of mass destruction, or towards salvation by boarding the 'ark' and remaining in the 'caravan'? How can humanity show solidarity, and traverse the desert peacefully? How can humanity's ark avoid sinking and survive the deluge?

I believe that the wager at the heart of all this is cultural, and not a bet on fickle politics governed by vested interests. Culture for me implies moral and social responsibility in domestic, foreign, national and international policies. All of humanity's know-how in governance, public administration, urban planning, resource management and investment in education and human development are but the fruits of constructive culture-focused development.

In addition to my career and the senior positions I have occupied in culture and diplomacy, the above is another reason why I believe the path to peaceful coexistence may only be achieved through culture, an idea I will further expand in the forthcoming chapters.

To me, the link between culture and diplomacy – one the basis of social peace and the other the basis of relations among nations – is the path to fostering collective thinking to save humanity's ark and caravan from being wrecked or losing its way. This book serves in part as a tour of culture and cultural diplomacy, which have much to offer by way of attaining a more secure and peaceful world.

Perhaps culture will serve as our dove bearing an olive branch, and will point us towards safe shores.

# Chapter One
## Doha: Localisation versus Globalisation

Sometimes we find ourselves in a position in which we must act out a script that we neither wrote nor developed. In such a situation, we must do what we have to do, play the part with self-confidence and perform to the best of our ability.

This is exactly what happened to me, as minister of culture, one day in 2009 on a live programme on Qatar TV involving viewers both in the studio and via telephone. The topic was preparations for Doha to serve as the 2010 Capital of Arab Culture.

I was there to answer questions from viewers. These questions were numerous and sometimes complicated, reflecting the strong interest of young people in particular in the year-long festivities, and their profound awareness of what needed to be done. They were very keen for the event to succeed in promoting Doha and her cultural achievements. It was also evident to me from their questions and comments that they had high hopes for the year, which put further pressure on me, there, live on air and in front of the public.

I had been appointed to lead the Ministry of Culture, Arts and Heritage, for the second time, in September 2008. Not long after, my ministry and I faced a great challenge: organising the Doha 2010 Capital of Arab Culture events.

There was little time to meet that imminent challenge. More challenging still was that this was happening in a country that does not believe in half-solutions or half-accomplishments. The boundless ambition of the country's leadership meant that it would accept nothing less than a resounding success.

There was no escaping it. Arab nations had approved the initiative unanimously and a date had been set. There was no way to postpone it or pull out, even though I did not even know where to begin to prepare for the big event. There was not even a hint of a programme. Worst of all, the infrastructure to host the series of events was neither ready nor adequate enough to meet the expectations of the leadership, which, after several years, had put me back in the top cultural post in the country.

When I went into the television studio that day, I had no idea of what kind of questions the public was going to ask. I was also not aware that the audience had been requested to submit answers to the question that was at the heart of my own concerns: Was Doha ready to be the 2010 Capital of Arab Culture?

I realised during the interview that what was at stake was successfully persuading the audience and viewers at home that the answer was 'yes', and to have confidence in the state and its resolve. My task was to inspire confidence in the Ministry of Culture, Arts and Heritage and its ability to achieve the success the public yearned for.

Yet, measured against what we knew at the time, organising a series of events that would meet such high expectations was a nearly impossible task. I had to delicately balance being sincere and creating the impression, as the person in charge of the events, that my team and I were ready to meet the challenge. But how does one convince people of anything based only on sincere intentions, in a world where the success of policies is measured with solid data and hard evidence?

That moment inspired me to try to address doubts and to emphasise our overwhelming desire to succeed.

I was, unquestionably, in a bind. Everyone, as it turned out, knew that preparations had yet to begin. Everything I told those young people came across to them as exaggerations unsupported by any real evidence. They were not convinced of my arguments about there being a strong will and ambition, despite all my efforts. However, I held on to my profound faith that we would succeed – and maintained a sense of calm that came from where I still do not know.

The polling soon ended and the answer of a majority of the audience was that Doha would not be ready in 2010 to serve as Capital of Arab Culture. More than 70 per cent had a negative answer.

By the standards of political communication, it was a disaster. I was not shocked, however, because what I knew supported the audience's conclusion.

The politician's role is to build on what is positive and inspire hope among people. So when the host asked me his most serious questions yet that day – 'Do you accept this challenge? Do you still believe Doha can be a successful culture capital?' – I answered confidently, 'Yes. I accept the challenge, and Doha will be one of the most successful capitals of Arab culture.'

This was not false optimism, despite the very real difficulty of my position and my failure to convince the audience and the viewers at large of my arguments. I drew my self-confidence from my intimate knowledge of the leadership's political will, its record in dealing with challenges and its keenness to always ensure perfect delivery. There was a rich record of achievements in this regard, and I would not have placed my expertise and credibility on the line if I had not myself been convinced of this.

Besides, I didn't have many options.

My team at the ministry and I had to roll up our sleeves and start working the very next day, although the reaction to what I had said on the programme was not enthusiastic. Many believed that we had taken a bigger risk than we should have done.

Today, when I recall some of those details, I have mixed feelings about those reactions. On the one hand, they added to the pressures that had piled up on me and my colleagues, driving me towards a certain frustration and despair. Doubts and fear of failure are very difficult. On the other hand, they served as an incentive to fulfil not a personal imperative, important as that may be for any politician entrusted with a difficult task, but, rather, a national, Arab and even human one.

Ultimately, my colleagues and I rose to the challenge and Doha succeeded brilliantly as Capital of Arab Culture.

Experience has taught me that success stems solidly from sincere political will. In the end, I was working with a leadership that never withheld the material or moral means for people to move forward and overcome difficulties.

## "Arab Culture Is Our Homeland, Doha Is Its Capital"

We had only a few months to get the job done. There were no departments in my ministry or in any other ministry which could supervise the forthcoming event, and the committee that would be formed later for the purpose did not yet exist.

I proposed to the cabinet that the prime minister chair this committee, and that I serve as his deputy. However, he insisted that I assume full responsibility and chair the committee myself. Again, this was something that acted as both a source of pressure and an incentive for me.

The first thing the committee did was to study the programmes of previous Arab culture capitals, to set a ceiling for expectations and to benefit from their experiences. Our goal was to distinguish ourselves with added quality and excellence.

I received many suggestions for a slogan for the event, many of which were appealing and memorable. In the end, I chose 'Doha, capital of the Arab culture homeland' as the slogan.

I chose it and proceeded to draft it delicately. I must say that we got it right with the slogan, as regards both its connotation and its phrasing. It truly captured the meanings and values we wanted to convey. Everyone who saw it was impressed right away. And to this day, it still reverberates in hearts and minds.

Doha Capital of Arab Culture was a chance for me, despite the sheer size of the responsibility and the urgency of what had to be done, to bring new thinking into an old issue related to culture. This was the issue of local versus global culture, which, like many cultural issues, was often raised in an antagonistic manner that almost forced one to take sides.

In truth, many aspects of this issue would not be raised were it not for the colonial legacy, the weak state of some societies and cultures, and the onslaught of globalisation. In addition, the context in which we live has brought a set of problems fundamentally linked to industrialisation and its impact on the cultural sphere, levelling many of the relics of the past caught in its path and the traditions of any given culture.

Generally, there is increasing tension between the local and the global, causing many latent fears to come to the surface. Many are concerned with the future of their local cultures, amid a flood of cultural goods and influences from every corner of the earth.

This is not strictly a phenomenon of the developing world. There are concerns even in some developed nations regarding so-called Americanisation and the threat of cultural homogenisation, prompting calls for cultural exceptionalism and cultural diversity.

The main concern behind all this is about surrendering to market logic when it comes to culture. Many nations have rushed to redouble their efforts to protect their cultures, while lobbying for a greater role by international organisations such as UNESCO and the WTO in safeguarding cultural diversity.

The great irony here is that globalisation's blitz against local cultures has been coupled with increasing calls emphasising indigenous cultural identity. It seems that our world is moving in opposite directions simultaneously: The more people come closer and move towards shared values and perceptions, the more there is a retreat into native identities and established traditions.

The obvious tension in the globalised cultural market has sometimes even led to extremist attitudes that promoted intolerance and threatened world peace. What is behind this kind of reaction is globalisation's tendency to impose on all cultures and lifestyles uniform values and to eliminate cultural distinctiveness.

## Can cultural particularities be wiped out?

A fair observer, however, will not readily accept appearances. A distinction should be made between globalisation, a fundamentally economic current with cultural implications, and global or universal values that are shared among cultures, no matter how far apart from one another they are or how strongly entrenched they are in their distinctiveness.

Reality seems to confirm that the continuous drive for modernisation by means of spreading certain cultural values from the West has not abolished distinctive cultural identities elsewhere. Indeed, despite the rapid erosion of some cultures, many of which were reduced to objects in museum displays, we also observe resilience among other solid cultures rooted in strong traditions that the globalised cultural market could not gobble up.

I see much evidence suggesting cultures have been able to absorb and assimilate the effects of industrialisation into their own respective contexts. The explanation behind this perhaps is that culture is not a set of inanimate goods consumed without leaving a mark. By its very nature, culture is averse to homogeneity and has great affinity for diversity and otherness. Meanwhile, cultures rooted in strong traditions can be flexible and adaptable in a way that makes them continuously shifting and developing, never quite coalescing into something permanent even if they sometimes appear to do so.

In this sense, many arguments advanced in the debate concerning the local versus the global seem to me erroneous and inconsistent with reality. People, as I see it, tend instinctively to emphasise their distinctiveness.

Furthermore, no one should claim that modernism, with its Western roots, is underpinned by an inclination to dress everyone in the same robe. Rather, one of the most distinguished traits of modernism is individuality and openness. Did modernism not rescue people from the vicious cycle that had made each individual an embodiment of behaviours their community chose for them? Did modernism not give individuals the ability to chart a path for their lives out of their own volition and awareness, and open their minds to potential opportunities that were not possible for them before?

The same goes for cultures.

From my own experience and observations of my country's culture, my Arab culture, and from my travels across five continents, experiencing their innumerable cultures, I came to see how each culture in its own way incorporates globalised cultural influences into its own specific context. Sometimes this process allows the old and the new to coexist. At other times, the two are merged and fused. And at others still, the new reshapes the old and presents it in a new form, or the new is incorporated into the old in a way that suggests it has always been part of a cultural tradition.

The same applies to how the particular and the universal, and the local and the global, interact. In effect, what I am arguing here is a logical consequence of the nature of culture in and of itself, should we contemplate it in a cool-headed manner.

We must forget about the technical definition of culture as the sum of knowledge, belief, art, morals, law, custom and any other capabilities and habits acquired by any one of us as a member of society. As important and as common as this definition may be, it does not explain the resilience of cultures in the face of the sweeping tide of globalisation.

I am not aware of any culture that, like mushrooms, grows outside of a social context rooted in history and geography. In that sense, culture is much more entrenched than we may imagine.

We should not be tricked by the might of the machine behind globalised culture. Cultures are quintessentially local, and they cannot be eliminated unless the societies that produce them disappear.

Yet at the same time, local cultures do not exist in isolation from historical shifts. They are not rigid and cannot afford to be so; in order to survive and thrive, cultures must accommodate changes and developments without losing their essential characteristics in relation to various practices, religious beliefs, cuisine, arts, leisure and so on.

What is unique to a culture that is socially entrenched and continuous is passed on from one generation to the next – otherwise known as tradition. For this reason, and no matter what time does to influence cultures, some, most or all of the components that set them apart survive in the collective mind and behaviour. In turn, this influences individuals and communities, and the cultural traits are reproduced naturally in this manner.

Here, I believe, lies the secret behind the endurance of diverse cultures, even if they converge or resemble one another. This sometimes hidden aspect is the solid foundation that gives us our frames of reference and the way we communicate within our societies and with others. No tendency towards homogenisation, regardless how strong, can supplant strong traditions that run through cultures, communities, individuals and personal behaviours, as blood flows in the veins.

Nothing is more indicative of this than the hard link between culture, language and identity. We take stock of our world through language, and communicate with other communities who are close to us through language, which makes us feel like we belong to a certain linguistic group. Language is the cornerstone of identity, as a symbolic representation of our social entity by which we delineate our cultural otherness and being.

## Let us build bridges

My team at the ministry and I embarked on the Doha Arab Culture Capital project based on this perception. I knew for certain that my country's culture had a solid core of traditions that would allow it to assimilate modernity in the best possible way, and had the flexibility to cope with cultural influences from all parts of the world.

I was fully aware that Arab culture, with its deeply rooted traditions, was in general robust enough to allow for a healthy interaction with world cultures without pulling up its roots.

We proceeded to hold consultations with our partners in literary, artistic and cultural circles for the opening ceremony. This was the event that was going to take us to all corners of the Arab cultural landscape, from the Gulf to the Atlantic, via the streets of Doha.

We chose the operetta *Bayt al-Hikma* (*The House of Wisdom*) for the opening ceremony, given its symbolism and the cultural connotations it carried, reflecting our position on dialogue and interaction among cultures. The intent was to strike a balance between highlighting our national culture and Qatar's arts, literature and heritage, and introducing our men and women, young and old, to other diverse cultures and arts.

Our firm conviction is that culture is the best way to become acquainted with others and to learn how to accept difference and embrace openness and tolerance. Cultural exchange also unlocks the potential for creativity, innovation and refinement thanks to artistic contact and intellectual interaction.

The Doha Capital of Arab Culture 2010 festivities were exceptional in the regional and international cultural scene. UNESCO, together with the Arab League, had launched the

Arab Culture Capital initiative with the aim of introducing and promoting Arab culture.

But Doha went further, wanting this series of events to celebrate all human culture and creativity. In addition to the Arab nations, scores of countries from all over the world participated in events, including the United Kingdom, France, the United States, Japan, Russia, China, India, Italy, Spain, Brazil, Tunisia, Kenya and other African and South American nations. In the course of the year, individuals and groups across the cultural spectrum visited Doha, showcasing their creativity in all areas: theatre, cinema, performance arts, photography, visual arts, literature and much more.

The Ministry of Culture, Arts and Heritage oversaw the festivities. When I sat with the team during the preparations for the events, we observed the richness of the artistic works of the countries we were planning to host. We asked fundamental questions about the best ways to communicate, interact and link all those diverse cultures. How should Arabic communicate with Hindi, Mandarin, English, French, Spanish, Russian and other languages?

The answer came to us clearly from the annals of history: translation and the dialogue of civilisations. The ancients, like those who came later, understood the value of translation and its crucial role in acculturation and the exchange of knowledge between cultures and civilisations. This was the rationale behind *Bayt al-Hikma*, established by Caliph al-Mamoun in Baghdad, as a centre of knowledge and translation.

Throughout human history, booms in translation activity coincided with radical cultural shifts. Scott Montgomery, in his treatise on the movements of knowledge through cultures and time, states, 'Between 1750 and 1860, translation constituted the vast bulk of scientific work, and it was wholly expected that most scientists would be translators first, before they were experimenters, field workers, or theoreticians. During this period, the idea of "contribution" in Japanese science meant, above all, increasing the library of its textual resources.'[2]

It is recognised in our time that there is no perfect linguistic equivalence among languages. Therefore, in the movement of knowledge between languages, the tension between source and target languages has led to a process of evolution adding to the knowledge contained in the original texts. An example of this, Montgomery writes, includes 'Ptolemy being given a monotheistic cast in Arabic, or Newton acquiring Confucian overtones in Japanese.'[3]

Since the Doha Arab Culture Capital festivities touched on these fundamental cultural issues, we decided to launch the event with an operetta inspired by the House of Wisdom. We wanted to emphasise the theme of acculturation, and, following the opening ceremony, we set up a dedicated space at the headquarters of the Ministry of Culture, Arts and Heritage with the same highly symbolic name as the operetta, the House of Wisdom.

One piece of wisdom relevant in the context of this cultural openness to the other comes from Irish scholar Michael Cronin's book *Translation and Globalisation*, a translation of which our ministry commissioned for the festivities. He wrote,

> It is precisely the fear of being annihilated, overpowered or undermined that can often dictate our attitude or conduct towards others. 'Do not talk to strangers' is a standard and valuable piece of advice imparted by parents, guardians and schools to young children. However, what may be protective of the world of childhood may become destructive of the world of adulthood if good counsel hardens into indifference or, more worryingly, intolerance.[4]

## *The House of Wisdom*: The rational knowledge society

Doha Arab Culture Capital 2010 launched with the brilliant operetta *The House of Wisdom*. The production's theme was the triumph of knowledge, intellect, arts and literature, as well as cultural exchange and the dialogue of civilisations as embodied by medieval Baghdad's House of Wisdom. The original House of Wisdom was founded on the basis of translation and discovery of other cultures. The purpose was to assimilate their knowledge and produce new knowledge, which would in turn enter the collective human consciousness, unimpeded by cultural or geographical barriers. The underlying message of the operetta was a call to revive this tradition.

As I once wrote, 'The House of Wisdom, founded by Caliph al-Mamoun, was a unique and pioneering experience reflecting the wisdom and awareness of decision-makers who appreciate the role of science in developing people and society, by creating, financing, and organising a climate conducive for this. The House of Wisdom was an effective launch pad for an astounding civilisation that benefited all of humanity for hundreds of years.'

The life of Caliph al-Mamoun is an important part of the play; since childhood, he had an unquenchable thirst for knowledge, believing that intellect is humanity's most treasured asset, and that knowledge is its main instrument. As caliph, he dedicated himself to establishing his signature centre of science – the House of Wisdom – that left an indelible mark on the Arab and Muslim world and beyond.

By examining the bulk of serious studies conducted on the House of Wisdom in various languages, we see how it was not just a huge translation project that was ahead of its time, but also a new vision to establish a rational knowledge society. We can add here the Arab League's view: 'The establishment of the House of Wisdom in Baghdad by the Abbasids was an extremely important cultural milestone in the history of the Arab and Islamic civilisation. It was not just a library, and a centre for translation, scholarship and debate. It was also a place for dialogue between the civilisations of the East and the West at the time, particularly the Arab-Islamic, the Greek, the Persian, the Syriac, and the Indian civilisations.'[5]

The House of Wisdom project allowed science and knowledge to flow between peoples and civilisations, and to spread in the Arab-Islamic dominion from the Gulf to the Atlantic, all the way to Andalusia and the Western world beyond it. Jim Al-Khalili, a British physicist, attests to this in his book *The House of Wisdom: How Arabic Science Saved Ancient Knowledge and Gave Us the Renaissance*.

Caliph Al-Mansour had founded the Khizanat al-Kutub (Book Depository) to store valuable manuscripts, but it was Al-Mamoun who converted it into the House of Wisdom. After all, a depository, no matter how large, is only a store without a soul, while a house refers to something full of life and activity. And, indeed, scholars from all cultural, scientific and linguistic backgrounds occupied this centre of knowledge and brought it to life.

Remarkably, in the present time, we see a similar trend in the function of national libraries, which have grown to become places of meeting and exchange, and not just book depositories. National libraries are today important national symbols, akin to the national flag or the national anthem.

National libraries such as the US Library of Congress, the Bibliothèque Nationale de France and the British Library highlight countries' investment in knowledge. In Qatar, we have a national library that houses many rare manuscripts and is equipped with cutting-edge technology.

Al-Mamoun understood that knowledge and science belong to all humanity, regardless of colour, race or creed. The function of the House of Wisdom was not to store books, be they original, copies or translations. It was to host a dialogue between civilisations that could overcome geographical, linguistic and ideological barriers.

## Boundless ambition

Our ambition behind Doha Arab Culture Capital 2010, after we assumed the challenge, proved sceptics wrong and reassured those who had concerns. But it went beyond the event itself, as important as it was. We wanted Doha to be truly a cultural capital recognised in the region and in the wider world. This motivated us to work hard to ensure that the capital had a well-developed and diverse cultural infrastructure, complete with museums, theatres, exhibitions and cultural districts.

## Katara and Souq Waqif

Doha has sustained its cultural activities over the years. Today, projects such as the cultural village in Katara represent a lifeline for culture, art and creativity, hosting Qatari, Arab and international events year round. Without exaggeration, Katara today is a global cultural edifice, and a space for diverse cultural happenings. Its charming location by the seaside at the heart of Doha also gives pleasure to the senses as well as fulfilling intellectual and cultural needs.

Though Katara cultural village was built in a traditional Qatari architectural style, its buildings are also inspired by other cultures. They include an opera and a Roman theatre. Katara's restaurants and cafés offer selections from diverse world cuisines. Above all, Katara has become a hive of creativity and a meeting place for writers and artists, who come to the cultural village from all parts of the Arab Gulf and the world.

Another cultural landmark in Doha is Souq Waqif, now a celebrated destination for locals and visitors, be they ordinary people or politicians, writers, artists, athletes or other celebrities. However, the souq's fame has to do with a secret not readily known except by those who are aware of the notion of culture in the broadest sense.

The souq was rebuilt using stones, gypsum and wood, materials that my countrymen and women have long used to ensure buildings were cool and airy in the hot and sometimes harsh climate of the Gulf. Yet the project did not rely solely on traditional Qatari architecture; all those who worked in and frequented the market – vendors, buyers, proprietors and visitors – were consulted and surveyed. People and their imaginations are more important than stones. The goal was not to build a monstrosity that people would ultimately shun. It was to build something culturally valuable that would be compatible with people's mindsets and at the same time serve its commercial function as a souq.

In short, Souq Waqif stands as a realistic example of the coming together of heritage and modernity, the fertile interaction between leaders and the public, and the desired intersection between art and daily life, without tradition standing as an obstacle to modernisation, and without modernisation ruining the tradition.

## On cultural enrichment

Doha's success as the 2010 Arab Culture Capital was a turning point in the history of cultural enrichment in my country, having firmly established awareness about the importance of culture and its social role. In reality, the event was part of a broad plan, the Qatar National Vision 2030, to create a knowledge-based society. The year-long celebration, like the various cultural achievements made by Qatar, was part of a clear vision for what is termed globally as 'culture-focused development'.

Individuals, leaders and countries today are all aware of the link between culture and development, though this might seem dubious at first glance. Indeed, culture in its simplest sense is a set of subjective values ingrained in individuals and their respective communities, while development, as something that requires planning, programmes and policies, is a more practical and

21

procedural concept. So how can something subjective be amenable to quantifiable development?

The apparent irreconcilability can be resolved by considering an institution such as the school as an incubator for developing intellect, talent, mindsets, culture and skills. Schools are subject to programmes, policies and planning aimed at shaping the future, and are proof that shaping people and their minds is not only possible but necessary.

Perhaps the most important achievement of modern educational institutions is that they have given broad segments of the community the opportunity to access knowledge. Are equal opportunities and broad participation not the very foundation of democracy?

This is the crux of the matter in my approach to culture-focused development. This practical concept expresses the effort to make culture accessible to all, by drafting policies that ensure cultural participation and easy access to information and knowledge.

There is an important underlying principle to this in modern societies, namely the need for continued extra-academic education and cultivation. Furthermore, culture-focused development cannot proceed in isolation from genuine democracy in the cultural field, where each individual is able to access culture and its products, through theatres, museums, libraries, exhibitions and the like.

In Qatar, we sought to take culture to the people in markets and streets, and to integrate it into their social and economic lives to break the vicious cycle that often makes culture the exclusive domain of the privileged few. This experience has paid off, with many ordinary people now included in the 'cultural cycle' that we have merged with the conventional economic cycle.

Our experience in this regard has been significant, based on including newer forms of art and cultural activities in the effort to revive, promote and preserve our heritage, combining modernity with tradition in a creative way in the Qatari context. Naturally, this has required a methodical approach and careful planning, building on successful experiences and best practices, so that culture would be present throughout the year in close connection to its human and physical surroundings.

This is how I understand culture-focused development in the social dimension. For me, it means giving individuals the chance to access culture and satisfy their needs for art, for meaning and for symbols that they can share with the community. It means improving the quality of life for all people in all aspects.

This cultural interaction between various aspects of daily life is one manifestation of what has been known for decades as comprehensive development, which integrates social, economic and culture-focused development. But the issue here is not about associating culture with economic development. Rather, reality shows that economic development almost automatically pushes forward culture-focused development without necessarily intending to do so.

To illustrate this, I suggest that factoring culture into comprehensive development does not stop at supporting cultural and artistic endeavours. It essentially and especially means that people, with their values and symbols, should be at the heart of comprehensive development, being both its engine and its intended recipient.

While economic and social development is measurable and has quantifiable indicators, comprehensive development is intrinsically linked to the human aspect of these results. The best expression of this human aspect is culture, as a set of discernible features of a given community.

For this reason, comprehensive development should combine qualitative and quantitative targets, beyond the conventional thinking regarding development issues, means and objectives. Culture is no longer a luxury or a distraction, but, rather, is a source of meaning and stability for modern human existence, giving a symbolic aspect to humans as producers without which people become mere machines or accessories thereto.

Developing culture is part of the overall welfare every development related undertaking seeks. One form of this welfare involves developing the creative capacities of individuals as well as establishing cultural services, allowing the community to discover its roots and individuals to form and interact with their surroundings in a rational, critical, open and communicative way. There is a noble goal behind this: namely, to alter individual and collective behaviour so that solidarity, harmony and hope will replace loneliness, loss and despair.

However, this understanding of culture and the way it should be developed alerts us to another important matter: that the intention is not just to allow talents to thrive and express themselves to enrich the moral, artistic and symbolic wealth of the community, but also to promote cultural democracy. Indeed, there should be a way to bridge the gap between the elite and the general public.

There is almost nothing as harmful to communities as having the cultivated elite and the public living in two separate worlds. For one thing, this leads to tyranny of the minority, which is left in control of the symbols of the community and of its cultural authority, in contradiction with cultural rights, a recognised human right in international charters and in any ethical consideration of comprehensive development.

By contrast, universal access to information and culture is a strong proof of the success of any development project. This goal achieves the desired balance between the creative elites and the general public, who are then able to interact with that elite to reaffirm its cultural identity and protect values, mores, traditions and beliefs no matter how strong the threats to them might be. In fact, such threats could in this way become incentives for introducing harmonious change and renewal into inherited cultural values, to bridge the gap between local cultures and global cultures, as well as between elitist culture and popular culture.

# Chapter Two
# The War on Heritage

## Holy ignorance and barbaric violence

In his film *Al-Masir* (*The Destiny*), the great Egyptian filmmaker Youssef Chahine portrays ignorant zealots burning books in the name of religion. While not the only film to contain such a scene, the episode Chahine portrays is especially appalling because its context is the decline of the Arab civilisation in Andalusia and of Ibn Rushd's enlightened ideas.

Ibn Rushd's ideas captured a brilliant moment in which Islamic thought intersected with Greek heritage to create a new global direction in philosophy. Chahine's scene captures well what extremism and zealousness may lead to, from intellectual insularity to barbaric violence against even books, as the vessels that host the ideas of thinkers and their creations.

One book I asked as culture minister to be translated contains many examples highlighting the relationship between ignorance and violence. *Books on Fire*[6] by Lucien Xavier Polastron shows how many people throughout history sought to extinguish the light of thought and stop the wheel of cultural history.

Just as creativity has existed in all cultures, so has obscurantism. The Inquisition in Europe in the Middle Ages is proof of this, and the list of books banned by the Catholic Church is but one chapter in this dark history.

In our time, book burning has been mostly replaced by censorship, a no less violent act. In the Arab and Islamic world, we are seeing a return to the primitive practice that falsely justifies itself with religious arguments. In reality, however, this phenomenon is linked to the destructive streak that usually accompanies conflict. The sabotage of human heritage during war and conflict is no less heinous than the ugliness of seeing people being tormented and left to face their fate alone, preyed upon by fear, disease and hunger.

## Syria on our mind

My interest in heritage is not limited to what I have mentioned in previous chapters, regarding the drive for modernisation in my own country. Indeed, Qatar has taken initiatives to help preserve human heritage beyond its borders.

In 2010, His Highness Sheikh Hamad bin Khalifa Al Thani, the Father Emir, instructed me to visit Homs to oversee efforts to restore its famous castle and the original Pact of Omar on display at the St Mary Church of the Holy Belt. This is one of the earliest known documents focusing on coexistence among different faiths. Homs is also home to rare historical religious sites: both St Mary's and the Khalid ibn al-Walid Mosque are masterpieces that carry many symbolic connotations. My visit to Syria would prove to be a farewell to a country I deeply love, before it was hit by devastation and war. Syria occupies a special place in my heart. I lived there for a few good years as ambassador, and developed relations of cordiality with and affection for its people. My diplomatic mission allowed me to closely understand Syria's strategic importance, but also experience its picturesque nature and the tolerance of its people, who held on to their shared culture and values, producing the famously diverse culture of the country.

It was in Syria that my eldest son Tamim was born. He drank from the water of River Barada and like me loved the land and its people. For this reason, I decided during that official mission to also visit various parts of Syria, whose devastation today breaks my heart.

I particularly wanted to visit Homs and Aleppo. When I assumed my post as minister of culture, arts and heritage for the second time, I found there were two files on the restoration of the Pact of Omar and the Homs citadel. Thus, I had to visit the two sites in question and check the progress of the works.

My visit to Homs started with the Ibn al-Walid Mosque. Khalid ibn al-Walid was also a brilliant military commander who helped expand the early Muslim state. His military achievements include the conquest of Syria, where he is buried inside the mosque that bears his name today in Homs.

The mosque was originally built in the thirteenth century AD before it was then rebuilt under Sultan Abdul Hamid II in the Ottoman style with a local Syrian twist, as those familiar with Islamic architecture no doubt know. The mosque is a masterpiece of Islamic architecture. It has nine domes of varying sizes, two magnificent minarets, three *mihrabs* and a marble pulpit. It is surrounded by a luscious green garden and contains a museum of Islamic art, in addition to the shrine of Khalid ibn al-Walid.

My heart breaks when I see online footage and images of what has happened to the resting place of the Prophet's companion and the mosque following relentless bombardment.

The Khalid ibn al-Walid Mosque and the tomb were not the only landmarks targeted by the barbaric violence of those seeking to take control of Homs and other cities. The devastation also hit the minaret of the Umayyad Mosque in Aleppo and parts of the old souqs in the ancient city.

I also visited the St Mary Church of the Holy Belt while in Homs. The church gets its name from the belt of the Virgin Mary, which it houses, preserved in a special shrine in an extension to the main building. Until a few decades ago, this church was the headquarters of the Patriarchate of Antioch and All the East of the Syriac Orthodox Christians, before it relocated to Damascus.

Built in the mid-first century AD, the church is one of the oldest in the world. It is a historic testament of the entry of Christianity into Homs and Damascus, and the persecution of the early Christians before Christianity became the religion of the empire. It is also a relic of ancient oriental church architecture, with its characteristic arches and arcades, and its stone masonry.

When I see the damage that has ravaged this historic landmark, I realise the extent of the criminal assault on history and heritage, and on coexistence between religions in a wonderful city like Homs. This coexistence would come to light particularly during the Prayers to Mary festival, usually attended by Syrians from different faiths: the faithful performed their rites and rituals, and members of other faiths would join them in the celebrations.

What the criminals want most is to efface the social order based on coexistence between religions in Homs and Syria in general. The irony is that the Muslims who ruled Damascus never tried to stop this ancient coexistence, but now these places and their Christian and non-Christian human heritage, which capture the tolerance and essence of Islam, are being destroyed in the modern era.

## The Pact of Omar

The Pact of Omar is an example of a long-standing culture of respect and coexistence among faiths and creeds in a framework of social peace. This age-old model emerged with the inception of the Islamic caliphate. It is as if the Pact of Omar had come from the depths of history to condemn what the extremists are perpetrating today against people, buildings and monuments across our Islamic world.

The Pact of Omar was a treaty signed between the Christian inhabitants of Jerusalem and the newcomer Muslims, safeguarding Christian rights and holy places in the city.

When we examine the text of the Pact of Omar, as Al-Tabari mentions in his chronicle, we read that the 'Commander of the Faithful' Omar bin al-Khattab pledges to give the people of Jerusalem 'an assurance of safety for themselves, for their property, their churches, their crosses, the sick and healthy of the city and for all the rituals which belong to their religion'.

> *Their churches will not be inhabited by Muslims and will not be destroyed. Neither they, nor the land on which they stand, nor their cross, nor their property will be damaged. They will not be forcibly converted.*
>
> *The people of Jerusalem must pay the taxes like the people of other cities [...]. The villagers may remain in the city if they wish but must pay taxes like the citizens [...]. Nothing is to be taken from them before their harvest is reaped.*

This document, which dates back roughly to 637 AD, was witnessed by four prominent companions of the Prophet: Khalid ibn al-Walid, Abdul-Rahman ibn Auf, Amr ibn al-Aas and Muwaiyah. It thus not only reflects the opinion of Caliph Omar alone, but also of the top Muslim commanders at the time.

We can see here the contrast between this humanitarian vision based on a moral approach to dealing with the members of other faiths, and those who have today been possessed by the devil of savagery and primitive logic. The claim by the criminal terrorists that they represent Islam is a lie behind which they hide their destructive tendency and their insular and ignorant understanding of a religion whose tolerance was established historically from the early days of the Prophet and his companions.

While the restoration of archaeological sites in Homs was a source of pride for me, and I was very keen to complete the project fully because of my sentimental relationship with Syria, its disruption in the wake of the Syrian Revolution since 2011 has been a source of great sorrow for me. Restoration works were converted into works of destruction, and in another sad irony, the Homs citadel became a military position.

To me, the burning of the St Mary Church of the Holy Belt and the levelling of graves and shrines are part of efforts by the ignorant to obliterate Syria's cultural and human mosaic.

Regardless of the details in this context, what is certain is that the sabotage of this human heritage dismays anyone who is aware of the value of this wealth, and denunciation and condemnation do little to change this.

## The destruction in Mosul

'When sorrows come, they come not single spies. But in battalions,' wrote Shakespeare in *Hamlet*. As I was revising the draft of this book, the battalions of ignorance were continuing their sacking of other world heritage sites in the cradle of civilisation, on the banks of the Tigris and Euphrates.

The news said a mob of marauders in Iraq had raided the ancient Assyrian city of Nimrud. They looted its treasures before bulldozing it.

Earlier, they had ransacked the Mosul Museum, destroying priceless statues and sculptures dating back to the Assyrian period. The mobs of ignorance brought down statues and destroyed them with sledgehammers and pneumatic drills. I do not discount the possibility that these mobs stole some artefacts to sell them to raise money for their terrorist activities, given the established link between smuggling and terrorism.

These events prompted UNESCO to describe what had happened as cultural genocide and a war crime. This was not metaphorical because what happened indeed amounts to a war crime. The city of Nimrud dates back to around 1300 BC, built by King Shalmaneser in the Assyrian middle period. In the ninth century BC, it was the capital of the world's most powerful empire. It was famous for its grand parks, magnificent gardens and majestic royal palaces, lined with various artefacts and giant statues, especially of winged bulls. All this suggests the Assyrians were a great civilisation.

The scant news emerging from Nimrud indicated the ignorant mobs razed the archaeological site to the ground. The site was home to a castle full of archaeological walls and statues. What is farcically atrocious is that those ignorant terrorists justified their actions by claiming they were destroying idols worshipped by the ancients.

This is a desperate pretext for people living outside history. They do not understand that those statues are testaments to a real history of human evolution and progress, until humanity reached the highest degree of monotheism. They do not understand that arts and architecture are testaments to a shared human civilisation that must be preserved just as we preserve the fundamental components of human life. But their cultural blindness has caused them to injure human culture in the heart.

The obsession with the purity of faith, when accompanied by ignorance of human history, arts and civilisation, becomes an instrument of destruction and sabotage against the essence of civilisation, and of values such as respect, humility and moderation.

## Timbuktu, the pearl of the desert

The adherents of 'holy ignorance' not only assaulted pre-Islamic human heritage, but also Islamic heritage itself. The city of Timbuktu in Mali is a glaring example of how the bulldozers of intolerance want to uproot the tree of human creativity and diversity, regardless of its cultural or religious roots.

Timbuktu, nicknamed 'the pearl of the desert', was a major centre of Islamic culture overlooking the African Sahara. Furthermore, it represented a cradle for many civilisations that passed through and left their marks there.

Timbuktu housed thousands of manuscripts, some predating Islam, shedding light on the history of religions, including Islam, in those lands, and the history of sciences in the Islamic period, including astronomy, medicine, agriculture and music. It was a veritable gateway to the proliferation of Islam and the knowledge of its people among the nations of Africa.

Timbuktu was a rich depository of history and culture. It is not surprising that the name of the city derives from a Tuareg word for an ancient profession some of their women pursued, 'the guardians of belongings and provisions'.

One day, this city woke up to an assault by the barbarians of the modern era, who carried out a massacre against its priceless heritage. Shrines, tombs and even mosques on the UNESCO World Heritage lists were destroyed.

The mobs of extremism destroyed the entrance of the ancient mosque of Sidi Yahya and removed one of its doors that people in the city believed should always remain closed. The criminals destroyed sixteen shrines in the city, which is called the City of Three Hundred and Thirty Saints, including the shrines of Sidi Mahmoud and Sidi al-Mukhtar, which were levelled with chisels and hoes.

It was an assault on the spirit and heritage of Timbuktu and the popular beliefs of its people who revered the shrines as part of their Sufi spiritual heritage.

## A final word: The ant and the elephant

I once wrote on my mobile phone the following musing: 'Humanity is astounding with its creativity that flows like a rumbling river! We cannot know where these tidal changes are taking us!'

This is not a compliment to humanity even if it deserves it. It is not a fear of the unknown even if fear is justified in a world developing at the speed of light and in part is ravaged by war and tragedy. There is something more profound behind this idea, a question about humanity's glaring contradictions.

Every day there are new gains surprising even those of us who are well prepared for surprises, against a terrifying creep of war, poverty, disease and ignorance. I am one of those who cannot understand how countries that claim to have limited financial resources and refrain from investing in the education of their children and youths, not to mention healthcare and basic social services, can still afford costly lethal weapons to wage dirty wars, including against their own peoples. What they spend could more than cover the funds needed to eliminate disease, poverty and ignorance in their territories.

We can justify and explain this using the terminology of regional and international politics, interests and intrigue, and use the theories of political science and strategic studies. But I am a strong believer in the idea that wars originate in the minds of human beings, and that we must therefore build forts for peace in their minds.

Peace for me is not just the end of war. It is an ideal that is much more profound and complex. There can be no peace as long as the trinity of death – poverty, disease and ignorance – remains firmly rooted and whose true danger wars and conflicts always reveal.

I do not need here to prove the existence of astounding human creativity. In fact, even as I write this page, there is a powerful proof before me: When I look at the digital tablet, I see the history of humankind and its latest innovations. I tap with my fingers on a polished screen and I find letters lining up, capturing my thoughts. I can easily go back and edit an idea, or reformulate it using one word in the place of another, or change an entire paragraph – all effortlessly.

When I remember the stages I had to go through, like many other citizens of the global village, to enjoy this amazing creation, I recall my suffering as a young boy who had to learn handwriting. Writing with a quill was cumbersome: One could puncture the paper; the ink could leak and smudge the script, or one's hand could slip and misplace a letter below or above the line. Learning to draw the Arabic script is difficult, and it took me a long time until it ultimately became as natural as my fingerprint.

I still find pleasure in writing with a pen, despite the temptations of technology. Like the rest of my generation, I transitioned from the quill to the pen and from the pencil to the fountain pen. Reed pens, which allow writing with a broad script, allowed me to experiment with my limited abilities in the art of Arabic calligraphy.

Everyone who has visited my personal library no doubt knows about my passion for collecting Quran manuscripts. The Quran is the medium where the genius of Arab and non-Arab calligraphers unfolded, where their spirit and creativity filled the script to leave their marks on the most illustrious book in the Arab Islamic culture. This is my greatest symbolic fortune, reminding me that I belong to the nation of the book whose first instruction to the Prophet and the believers was to read.

While the Qurans I have collected are a selection of some of the greatest works of the foremost Arab and Muslim calligraphers, my favourite is the one that belonged to my father. This Quran was written in the script used in the Urdu language in the Indian subcontinent. It is a strange and captivating cross between the sacred Arabic text and a script invented by a people who speak a different language, an exhilarating image of trans-culturalism.

The coexistence between the pen and the digital tablet, and between marvellous scripts in the Qurans in my library and the collections of fonts on computers and mobile phones, eases some of the apprehension I feel regarding the sudden transformations taking place in the world. What I see is not a break but an accumulation in evolved intelligence, in digital form today.

Likewise, humanity transitioned from the Sumerian tablets of Mesopotamia to digital tablets today. In the intervening eons, humankind spent centuries developing writing mediums, from the invention of paper in China to the formalisation of the alphabet in Phoenicia in the first millennium BC. It took humanity many more centuries to invent the printing press and develop printing and binding techniques.

Digital books, in addition to the revolution they started in publishing and distribution, have become a container that can also accommodate old printed books and manuscripts. The huge storage capacity means the great challenge of digitising manuscripts can be eventually overcome to preserve human heritage and provide access everywhere and in all languages.

This amazing development stems from centuries of evolving human knowledge, which is today at risk because of wars that destroy the essence of humanity and the roots of its creativity.

What has happened in Timbuktu, Syria and Iraq, and in other countries where human heritage and monuments are being assaulted, confirms that the road to peace and goodwill between people is still long. No matter how serious and grand our efforts are in preserving heritage, they are like ant steps in the face of wars in which the elephant steps of mobs of sacred ignorance can destroy all progress.

Yet the creative and diligent ant must continue its work despite the risk of being crushed by elephants.

# Chapter Three
# An Aesthetic Exploration
of the World

## Literature

I must admit that my early entry into the world of diplomacy, along with my traditional background, tinged my relationship with knowledge with a patina of expediency and pragmatism. For part of my life, a good book was a book that taught me something new, or something that would help me see things differently. A good book was one that offered me a different angle or raised an issue that required mental effort on my part to resolve. In my early development, this for me was useful knowledge that would lead to useful work. For this reason, reading to me was a demanding journey into knowledge and ideas that implied I always had to come back with spoils.

I was thus keen to select the books I read very carefully, looking for something that would enrich the means by which I approached reality, analysed it and deciphered it.

Things were different for me, however, when I was a student at Cairo University. Arab novels played an exceptional role in my life, not least because my student years happened to coincide with a great moment for culture. At the time, Cairo was a hub of cultural activity, with great writers such as Tawfiq al-Hakim, Mahmoud Abbas Akkad, Mahmoud Timor, Yahya Hakki, Ihsan

Abdulkuddous and Youssef al-Sibai, to mention but a few. Naturally, Naguib Mahfouz was the leading man of that zeitgeist, but I want to write about him in detail when I tackle literature and the Nobel Prize.

In truth, my habit of selecting only books that I felt I needed, after reading their titles and skimming their contents, forewords and afterwords, rarely caused me disappointment. I maintained this kind of relationship with books, and then I was fortunate to meet someone who forever changed my outlook on knowledge.

God ordained that I marry a woman who is extremely passionate about reading. She devours books one after the other, always keeping up with the newest contemporary Arabic novels and the best of world literature. She has been like this ever since I first met her, and no preoccupations of life, new forms of media and their temptations, or digital fads and innovations ever managed to change her reading habits. She is always thrilled by what she reads, eager to share with me her impressions on the world of novelists, their tales and their style, until I have come to blindly trust her refined literary taste forged by the years and the pages she has read.

I have seen the influence of her readings clearly in her delicate attention to detail and in the way she perceives things, people and everyday business. I also admit that at first I saw the novels she read as mere leisure and recreation. Literature to me meant the poetry and prose of classical Arab works, which contain immortal wisdom and noble values that cultivate and educate a person. The genre of the novel, which is fairly recent in Arab culture, was to me little more than entertainment and not part of what I saw as a source of useful knowledge. To me novels were hardly more than the fantasies of characters drawn from the imagination, jotted down by authors to lure in readers without the promise of any practical benefit.

I thought for a period of time that books, as vessels of knowledge and carriers of value, fell under two mutually exclusive categories:

enriching, worthwhile books and entertaining, fictional books. However, thanks to my wife Zainab, these two categories have intersected, and she soon encouraged me to take up novels. I was drawn to them afterwards until my attitude towards them changed gradually from apathy to love and fondness for the genre.

My wife Zainab would often read to me a paragraph that had attracted her attention or invite me to consider a book she was reading. One day, I found myself drawn to read a historical novel. I saw how the book combined useful knowledge – history – with the smooth and fresh style that marks refined literature and fiction, reconstructing past events in a novel way.

## The thin line

Among the important aspects of the historical novel that caught my attention, having read a number of different ones by authors such as Jurji Zaydan and Ben Salem Himmich, is the relationship between history and storytelling. This encouraged me to organise a seminar on this very subject at the Culture Salon of the Ministry of Culture, Arts and Heritage, attended by Moroccan novelist Ben Salem Himmich himself. Arab countries have produced great historical novels, too numerous to list, by prominent writers from the Mashreq and the Maghreb.

This genre of writing became one of my intellectual and literary fixations, which is why I thought it would be a good idea to share it with the public and start a debate about any issues surrounding this genre. The question that always occupied me was this: What is the thin line between history and fantasy? Each time I read a historical novel, I asked myself: Did this historical character really think along those lines? Did characters really do this or did the writer attribute to them things that they did not in reality do?

The questions were simple on the surface, a sign of one being immersed in the novel and its charming universe. But in my opinion the questions hide a bigger issue: Do historical novels serve history by teaching a broader audience about certain historical epochs or figures, or do they create an alternate history different from the real one?

Arab writers, like other writers, still confound history with fantastic narration of history, a feature of the works of Jurji Zaydan, the pioneer of the Arab historical novel. Scholars agree that some of his novels, at least, turned non-factual fantasies into historical facts in the minds of his readers. So how is the historical novel received exactly? What if the reader were to believe that what he is reading is factual history? Would that not turn historical fiction into historical fact in his or her mind?

Historical novels are no exception to questions of literary and artistic creativity. But they require profound knowledge, culture and experience, and a spiritual willingness to interrogate different epochs and places.

In this regard, Himmich's view is based on a well-argued premise that history, as a science or an art in various cultures, emerged as the narration of a story revolving around a given event. That is, the relationship between history and the novel is deeper than we might imagine at first glance. Interestingly, the Greek historian Herodotus is considered the first person to experiment with historical fiction, so much so that the famous Roman orator Cicero nicknamed him both 'the father of history' and 'the liar'. To be sure, Herodotus resorted to lies when he was short of facts, and when he embellished stories to keep the reader interested.

In the Arab-Islamic culture, we know that ancient books, such as the history of the creation of the world and humanity and the narratives of the prophets and messengers, are not without fantastic stories about marvels and supernatural events that defy reason and logic.

Some books in our heritage inspired by historical figures belong to this fantasy genre in a way, including the stories about Antara,

Saif bin Abi Yazan, Zahir Baybars, and the epic Taghribat Bani Hilal. The same can be said of books about dreams, wonders, miracles and adventures.

I have recalled this rich Arab narrative history for a number of important reasons. The connection to heritage and history for the Arab writer and poet is central. As I wrote, 'Arab heritage is the natural milieu for this writer or poet's linguistic and creative acquisition, and heritage is a defining backdrop and reference frame for fictional characters and their emergence in the world ... those who do not understand this connection may be susceptible to subscribe to an inconsistent modernity or irresponsible, and loose nihilism.' This is one response to the European central hypothesis that assumes the novel as a genre only emerged with Cervantes and Don Quixote.

There is a broader vision that makes us see heritage and history in everything. As Carlos Fuentes once suggested, every novel becomes over time historical. It answers time, or rather creates it. The most significant stories are those that create rather than just reflect times. There is no such thing as a non-historical novel. There is no work of art or literature positioned outside time, outside history.

Nothing is more indicative of this than the experience of the Arab literary genius and Noble Prize winner Naguib Mahfouz. In what critics called the Pharaonic novels – especially *The Struggle of Thebes*, *Mockery of the Fates* and *Rhadopis of Nubia* – Mahfouz used history as a setting in which events, relationships and characters take shape, interact and evolve. When Mahfouz moved to his so-called social realism novels, with books like *Cairo Modern* and the Cairo Trilogy – *Palace Walk*, *Palace of Desire* and *Sugar Street* – these quickly became historical novels in the sense that anyone who wants to learn about contemporary Egyptian history has to read them.

In fact, people's need for the fictionalisation of history has to do with something profounder still. Novels make it possible to dig deeper into issues that history otherwise keeps mum about: the emotional and psychological state in the daily lives of various social classes, since usually formal history only approaches this timidly if at all.

Though ignored by historians, these personal, subjective realms are a source of abundant material for historical novels and a fertile ground for imaginative writing. Imagination is the instrument for the writer and the reader of the historical novel to fill the gaps between reality as incompletely described by historians and actual history and its complex layers and possibilities. Historical novels, when constructed tightly and given a focus by an honest, reverential writer, are no less valuable than history books when it comes to shedding light on deep historical and human truths.

Writers who have a penetrating imagination and nuanced knowledge of human psychology, and who are adept at imagining characters and situations, are also able to present history in an intellectually palatable, enjoyable and engaging form.

Again, this is a place where aesthetics and ethics interact to produce both benefit and entertainment, and where we can see ourselves reflected in the mirror of human history and its fickleness and suffering, but also its yearning for freedom and emancipation.

Whatever can be said about novels – particularly historical novels – can be said about television dramas, too, especially those set against a historical backdrop. In truth, television dramas have a stronger impact because they influence a broader audience. Indeed, dramas are watched not only by the cultured minority but by a broad segment of viewers of various backgrounds.

In many cases, historical dramas are people's only source of information about history, particularly those who have not received extensive education. In the Arab world, if not the world at large, the general public accounts for the overwhelming majority of people.

To cite one example of many, I remember the serialised drama *Harem of the Sultan*, a Turkish series dubbed into Arabic that was a major commercial success among Arab viewers. The series centres on the life of Suleiman the Magnificent, one of the most prominent Ottoman sultans, depicting him as a womaniser surrounded by concubines, with no preoccupation other than the women in his palace and their scheming and intrigue.

However, historical evidence indicates that Suleiman the Magnificent was the second Ottoman caliph, Commander of the Faithful and the first sultan to rise to power peacefully. Since he was one of the sultans most committed to law, or what we call today the rule of law, he was nicknamed Suleiman the Magnificent, or Suleiman the Magnificent to the European powers of his day.

Suleiman rarely made a decision without first obtaining an edict and was a great conqueror under whose reign the caliphate doubled in size. He continued to take part in battles well into old age, and died at the age of seventy-six in what is present-day Hungary.

During his reign, he built one of the largest mosques in the empire, the Süleymaniye Mosque, named after him. Beyond its refined internal aesthetics and external architecture, the mosque's ingenious design takes into account acoustics to ensure prayers and sermons reach the thousands of worshippers who attend it.

According to some accounts, the sultan's heart was removed after his death and was buried where he fell in Hungary during the Szigeth expedition. This explains why he has two graves one in Hungary where his heart and internal organs are buried and another in Istanbul for his body. Yet despite this heroic history, thanks to *Harem of the Sultan*, many people may only remember him as a man who devoted all his time to concubines and harem!

I visited Istanbul in late 2014, touring Topkapi Palace, or the Istana. By then, I had already watched the last episode of *Harem of the Sultan*. I remember imagining meeting Sultan Suleiman in one of the corridors of the palace. I imagined him to be very angry and annoyed because of the way he had been portrayed in that series. I heard myself telling him that history had been kind and fair to him, and asking him why he was upset. I imagined him retorting: 'People in your world today do not read and instead learn their history from television series. Be fair to me and let people know the truth!' When I returned to Doha, I wrote this on my Instagram.[7]

Returning to the art of the novel, my perception thus changed of fictional entities created by the ink of imagination. I found out through them that this great art probes in a unique way into human psyche and mood and into the details of human life and its twists and turns – changing our perception of things, of life and of human beings. I added fiction to my list of beneficial knowledge. Reality is sometimes stranger than fiction, but fiction is the best lens into reality.

Most certainly, the dialectic of novels and factual history will continue to be a topic of debate for scholars and aficionados of literature, a debate that will be difficult to settle.

I realised that literature is much more serious than I originally thought. It removes the nesting dolls hidden in the folds of the human psyche and uncovers mysterious layers of our existence, be they layers of nobleness and impossible perseverance, or layers of baseness and villainy.

Literature provides us with the kind of knowledge about people that scientific concepts and reasoned analysis may not be able to fully grasp or capture. Literature seems to have a secret way of making readers feel joy, sadness, sympathy or antagonism, and identity with characters and metaphors in full or in part.

My next confession is that my passion for literature means that I wait eagerly each year for the announcement of France's Prix Goncourt as well as the Noble Prize in Literature. These two prizes – regardless of the debate and controversy they often spark in the French and international literary scenes – offer a rare opportunity to discover writers.

Because of this personal interest, as minister of culture, I took the initiative and asked a department at the ministry to acquire Arabic translation rights for the speeches of Nobel literature prize laureates. My intention was to introduce the Arab readers to some of the experiences of prominent international writers and the revelations they shared in their acceptance speeches.

I was keen for the translations to be of superior quality, befitting the texts of those great men and women. With the same enthusiasm, we celebrated the first edition of the Arabic translation by inviting Professor Kjell Espmark, president of the Nobel Committee for Literature, to Doha. For the first time in the Arab world, he delivered a lecture to an audience of Qatari and Arab intellectuals and members of the public, on the criteria and the process the committee uses to vet and select candidates and winners, and gave a brief overview of its history and evolution.

When I met Professor Espmark in my office at the ministry, to honour him personally and the institution he represented, I found him to be modest, kind and wise, his wisdom shaped by years of experience in refined debate. Our conversation about literature and culture in Qatar and the world covered many topics and views, but I remember to this day two key ideas my guest, who was not a talkative man, expressed simply and spontaneously.

First, his impression of Doha was interesting. It was his first visit to my country, and he was astonished by the whiteness everywhere, including the traditional white thobe that we wear and always keep clean, pure and pressed.

Secondly, in the course of our conversation, he used an interesting metaphor. He said culture is a seed that must be sown each year to yield a bountiful harvest of meaning and beauty. If for some reason there is a drought, people who are wise would rather go hungry if necessary, rather than eat those seeds, so as to preserve them for future generations. Otherwise, future generations will have no seeds of culture to plant, so to speak.

## Nobel Lectures: Aesthetics and ethics

One of the pleasures of reading the *Nobel Lectures in Literature* is discovering the secrets they reveal about writing and writers. They also express the ideals behind the prize and the winners' affirmation of them, despite the various interpretations of the 'ideal direction', a phrase alluded to in Alfred Nobel's will. That idealism is a human vision, an expression of commitment to universal causes and an ethical position captured in beautiful language.

The idealism also seeks to strike a creative balance between ethics and aesthetics, and it is not unusual for the lecturers who speak before the Nobel Committee for Literature to underscore this combination.

Joseph Brodsky (Nobel Prize, 1987) went so far as to consider aesthetics to be the mother of ethics. If in ethics not 'all is permitted', it is precisely because not 'all is permitted' in aesthetics, he announced. The Peruvian novelist Mario Vargas Llosa (Nobel Prize, 2010) asserted, 'A literature stripped of morality is in human'. The author can never overcome his humanity, he added, in his quest for freedom and to wave the Utopian banner high.

In my opinion, most lectures for receiving the Nobel Prize in Literature revolve around these two themes.

On the one hand, writers highlight what Anthony Burgess calls 'the aesthetic exploration of the world'. There is a tendency among novelists to write what Günter Grass calls 'our shared story' with, in the words of Kenzaburō Ōe, a 'humanist view of man'.

These novelists transcend barriers and time, drawing the features of what Camilo José Cela calls the 'universal human'. The profound feeling of 'global citizenship' analysed by Mario Vargas Llosa stems from this view. 'We should not confuse a blinkered nationalism and its rejection of the other, always the seed of violence, with patriotism, a salutary, generous feeling of love for the land where we were born,' Llosa said.

On the other hand, the Nobel laureates underscore the importance of literature as a source of hope, and as a way to preserve and affirm life through linguistic devices. Literature can express the essence of humanity and forge a universal language out of the vocabulary of human suffering and yearning for freedom.

Storytelling is, in fact, one of the features of civilisation, as the birth of language coincided with the birth of communication – and fiction. Storytelling was a long journey thereafter, during which our humanity evolved. Storytelling gave people shelter from the mysterious, unfathomable world and its dangers, like a 'cool bath, a quiet pool for those spirits always on the alert'. From the time they began to dream collectively, to share their dreams, 'their life became dream, pleasure, fantasy, and a revolutionary plan: to break out of confinement and change and improve, a struggle to appease the desires and ambitions that stirred imagined lives in them', as Llosa declared.

Two of the qualities intricately linked to this ethical and aesthetical endeavour, and which are evident to readers of the Nobel lectures, are modesty and commitment. Joseph Brodsky, for instance, mentions that many of the poets and novelists he alluded to are more talented than him and have more to say to the world than he does. Claude Simon said that other writers in France and beyond deserved the prize, perhaps more so than he did. In turn, Portugal's José Saramago paid tribute to the stories of his grandfather and their ghosts, terrible tales and quarrels, while Le Clézio recalled his maternal grandmother's stories. Italian playwright Dario Fo praised his town's storytellers and glassblowers, to whom he said he owed a huge debt, for teaching him and other children the art and craft of spinning fantastic tales.

In addition to reflecting an ethical position, the modesty that characterises great writers expresses something more profound: namely, that they sense they are contributors to a human symphony extending from the first storytellers in the caves to the ordinary people who teach us everything to the great writers in all cultures. A true author is someone who overcomes his or her sense of self-importance as a talented person and any kind of a solipsistic sense of narcissism.

## Hunger and the banquet of knowledge

One paradox for authors, according to Le Clézio in his Nobel lecture, is that they can only address peers who know how to read and write. Those excluded, he said, must be 'magnanimously invited to the banquet of culture', and those who did not have the chance to learn to read ought to have the chance to read what novelists write.

Although writers may dream of changing attitudes, minds and hearts through the stories and universes they create, as a first step towards changing reality and the world for the better they often find themselves to be little more than witnesses.

Bearing witness as such is especially relevant in light of the tragedies and injustices of our time. The paradox of being, according to Günter Grass, lies in hunger and food shortages amid outrageous abundance, where gluttony coexists with famine and hunger turns into misery.

In his lecture, Dario Fo alluded to trials and massacres and bombings in public squares. Nigerian playwright and poet Wole Soyinka recalled the legacy of colonialism and the exploitation, persecution, racial arrogance and blatant hypocrisy associated with it. The humans behind that legacy wasted huge resources to purchase and develop armaments instead of building schools, libraries and hospitals.

Le Clézio was right when he said that effacing illiteracy and resisting famines were strongly linked.

In my opinion, the correlation between combating illiteracy and hunger sums up a key aspect of human tragedy on our planet as expressed by many of the lecturers at the Swedish Academy.

Doris Lessing, winner of the 2007 Nobel Prize in Literature, recalled her yearning and thirst for books in north-western Zimbabwe despite the rough conditions of life there. People would tell her: 'Please send us books when you get back to London.' Meanwhile, a teacher at a very good school in north London told her: 'You know how it is. A lot of the boys have never read at all, and the library is only half used.'

Lessing noted: 'A good paperback from England costs a month's wage in Zimbabwe.' She worked with a civil society group to bring books to the African nation, where she was greeted with tears. Although the library in the village where she went was 'a plank on bricks under a tree', it was a formidable resource for literacy classes, which she described very aptly as 'citizenship classes'.

This was another invitation to the 'banquet of culture', to use Le Clézio's phrase again. It is not just that writers do not come from homes where there are no books, as Lessing said, but also that equality and respect for others cannot be ingrained without giving every child the benefits of writing and reading. The child who reads and writes, according to Le Clézio, carries inside him the future of humankind.

Yet the issue is not just about an elite's desire for every person on this planet, especially in developing nations, to access the privileges of reading and writing, but also about a universal view that culture belongs to all of humanity. This is why some Nobel literature lecturers assign great value to books as a means to propagate culture. Books are a simple instrument that do not require the kind of high expenditure associated with modern technologies, and yet books remain a luxury in many parts of the world.

Whatever the case, there are many solutions to the problems of publishing and distribution that require only an honest will, in order for literature to be this 'wonderful tool for self-knowledge, for the discovery of others, and for listening to the concert of humankind, in all the rich variety of its themes and modulations'. As Le Clézio further declared, this means that culture on a global scale concerns us all, or at least it should.

While authors may experience what Turkish writer Orhan Pamuk describes as 'the fear of being left outside, the fear of counting for nothing, and the feelings of worthlessness that come with such fears – the collective humiliations, vulnerabilities, slights, grievances, [and] sensitivities', they are emboldened by the fact that they help resist universal oppression, the multifaceted form of inhumane humiliation which crossed over from the twentieth century to our present century. But literature, like all forms of human creativity, is a permanent quest for 'triumphing over errors ... when man has had time to lick his wounds and listen again to the urgings of his spirit', as Soyinka put it. And as Nadine Gordimer said, perhaps there is no other way to understand being except through art, and the entryway to art is reading and writing.

For the Nobel lecturers it is clear that ignorance and injustice are synonyms. Both are due to human arrogance; 'man stopped respecting himself when he lost the respect due to his fellow-creatures,' said José Saramago. Literature's role is to constantly emphasise humanity's universal ordeal, a fact that is often lost on many.

The problem is that the line splitting our joint humanity between 'enemies' and 'allies' has come to resemble 'the net on a tennis court', according to Irish poet Seamus Heaney, 'a demarcation allowing for agile give-and-take, for encounter and contending'.

# The spirit's calling

This specifically highlights the singular role of literature in building bridges between people. By making us enjoy and suffer and feel surprise, literature unites us beneath the languages, beliefs, habits, customs and prejudices that separate us; it is a protest against the insufficiencies of life, according to Llosa. 'Without fictions we would be less aware of the importance of freedom for life to be liveable,' he said. The absence of literature from the world would make it 'a world without desires or ideas or irreverence, a world of automatons deprived of what makes the human being really human: the capacity to move out of oneself and into another, into others, modelled with the clay of our dreams'.

This is how literature and life are interconnected; literature is therefore a necessity and not an aesthetic frivolity. Orhan Pamuk even stated his belief that literature is 'the most valuable hoard that humanity has gathered in its quest to understand itself'. 'Societies, tribes, and peoples grow more intelligent, richer, and more advanced as they pay attention to the troubled words of their authors,' he added.

Literature's ability to transcend ideologies, national borders and ethnic and linguistic barriers has to do with something fundamental: 'Man's existential condition is superior to any theories or speculations about life,' declared Chinese Nobel laureate Gao Xingjian (2000). Literature to him is a universal observation on the dilemmas of human existence, where writers strive to present the truth and bear witness to people's ordeals and their causes.

Literature, truth, intellect and freedom are thus intricately linked. Literature, which combines aesthetics with ethics, gives us the ability to resist fearing those who want to take away our freedom, which we gained during the long, heroic march of civilisation. This clinging to freedom, as a horizon for literature, humanity and civilisation, gives us confidence 'in the superiority of human freedom and dignity', as Camilo José Cela said.

A writer's ethical commitment to truth does not mean he or she should be content with the role of witness, however. Literature has an extraordinary ability to shape views by, in Llosa's words, 'creating a parallel life where we can take refuge against adversity, one that makes the extraordinary natural and the natural extraordinary, that dissipates chaos, beautifies ugliness, eternalises the moment, and turns death into a passing spectacle'.

Though this, according to Llosa, depicts life in a misleading way, it makes it easier for us to understand and compensates for the repression and uncertainty we go through in real life. It is a creative energy that 'introduces into our spirits non-conformity and rebellion, which are behind all the heroic deeds that have contributed to the reduction of violence in human relationships'.

Günter Grass corroborated this idea in his distinguished lecture. To him, 'narration is a form of survival' as well as a form of art. We may add, based on the testimonies of others in the Nobel lectures, that literature is more than that.

Saramago turns ordinary people into literary characters who resist oblivion, and glorifies the monotony of daily life, creating a memorable world where he would like to live from imagination. Orhan Pamuk, when he imprisons himself in a room for hours writing about his personal yet somehow universal wounds, shows great confidence in humanity, which he addresses through literature.

These different perceptions of literature and its role in the lives of people and societies are proof of the complex and multidimensional nature of literature. One of the reasons for this is the creative correlation between style and substance, that is, aesthetics and ethics. If a writer focuses on only one of the two, it may lead him or her into the trap of pompousness and vacuity, or to preaching and ideological bias. What is meant by commitment therefore is to find ways to produce writing that is both aesthetically pleasing and moving, and that expresses the suffering, contradictions and pains of humanity as it discovers itself and the world, and as it seeks and yearns for freedom in a grand existential story. Writing that tells the ultimate story of humans, creators of civilisation, meanings, and values that reflect the essence of their being and the calling of their spirits.

Just as biology shows the diversity of humanity within its universal character, literature is as diverse as the human themes it tackles within its universal meaning. This is the lesson I learned from the Nobel literature lectures. They showed me once again, despite my practical and pragmatic disposition, that what once appeared to be mere leisure and fantasy is much more serious and profound than I ever imagined. Literature tells the truth and fertilises imaginations, and charts paths for work and action.

## The groan and the call

I would like to turn to two Nobel lectures for reasons that, while personal, are linked to my cultural and diplomatic position.

The first lecture is by Naguib Mahfouz, 1988 laureate, and the only Arab to win the Nobel Prize in Literature. I grew up reading his charming narrations and exhilarating novels, having lived a period of my formative years in Cairo, the city whose secrets, charms, alleyways and neighbourhoods provided the setting for most of Mahfouz's novels.

The second lecture was delivered by Octavio Paz from Mexico, a fellow diplomat known for his poetry and broad culture, though I must admit that we do not share the same ideas on all issues, particularly politics.

Naguib Mahfouz's lecture was perhaps the briefest Nobel lecture of them all. Nonetheless, it held to the same universal themes, grounded in the cultural context of an Egyptian novelist whose work is deeply rooted in the civilisation of ancient Egypt, who is an Arab member of the pan-Islamic civilisation, who is a Third World citizen burdened with difficulties and challenges, and who is a humanist who, as he put it, drank the nectar of the rich and fascinating Western culture.

Naguib Mahfouz did not emphasise ancient Egyptian empire-building and conquest as an achievement because modern conscience no longer welcomes those feats. He did not stress the ancient Egyptians' discovery of monotheism, an achievement covered by others at some length, or their arts and architecture, again known to many people who have seen them firsthand or read about them. Rather, Mahfouz's novels were about truth and justice in an ancient Egyptian setting because these are more telling of the superiority of a civilisation than any riches or splendour, as he said.

Mahfouz spoke about the distinguished qualities of the Islamic civilisation, which calls for humanity to unite under the guardianship of the Creator, in an atmosphere of freedom, equality and tolerance. He told the story of an Islamic commander who traded prisoners of war with Byzantium in return for books on ancient Greek philosophy, medicine and mathematics. He concluded that Muslims' faith does not stop them from seeking knowledge even when it is the fruit of a 'pagan culture'.

Naguib Mahfouz did not stop at the past and its eternal values, but also tackled his present time, many of whose problems still exist today. He spoke about debt, famine, racial segregation, human rights violations and the injustice visited upon the Palestinian people.

As Mahfouz put it, these are the 'groans of mankind' in the age of civilisation as humanity enters adulthood. More importantly, the leaders of the ancient world worked for the good of their own nations, seeking superiority, dominance and glory, while civilised leaders today are responsible before all of humanity. Mahfouz thus proclaimed that we are living in the age of leaders responsible for the entire planet.

Naguib Mahfouz's lecture was both a 'groan' and a 'call': the groan of a large part of humanity suffering from tyranny, hunger, debt and spiritual pollution; and a call for shouldering jointly the responsibility to uphold high human values and spread good to counter evil and wicked people.

Naguib Mahfouz's groan will continue to resonate around the world as long as its causes exist, and his noble call remains valid a quarter of a century on.

## On modernity and tradition

I would like to analyse the lecture of my fellow diplomat Octavio Paz, which he delivered two years after Naguib Mahfouz. Paz reminded me of the years I served as a non-resident ambassador in Latin America, based in New York. He also reminded me of my years as my country's ambassador to France where he also served as ambassador.

The first thing that drew my attention was his talk about a cultural dialogue unfolding in the arena of languages and civilisations. As he said, languages are vast realities that transcend the political and historical entities we call nations.

As soon as I arrived in France, I found myself hurrying to learn French. I also sought to quickly improve my English as soon as I settled in the United States. It was not just about mastering a key requirement of diplomatic work, but also about taking a deeper stance related to having closer access to the cultures that speak these two languages and enjoying the fruits of their intellectual, literary and artistic achievements. Thus, my Arab identity and universal identity interacted without acrimony or contradiction, as Octavio Paz said.

I am of the view that the configuration of cultural relations among us Arabs is similar to that found in the Mexican culture, in that they appear as though built on emotion, perhaps distinctly from the European tradition. The consciousness of being separate, as Paz said, thus seems to be a feature of our 'spiritual history'. This feeling causes tension and constant self-examination, as much as it incites us to 'go forth and encounter others and the outside world'.

Interestingly, Paz sees this self-awareness as an existential condition that prompts us to probe our unfathomable depths to render our ventures and exploits, and our acts and dreams, 'bridges designed to overcome the separation and reunite us with the world and our fellow beings'.

Paz presented some manifestations of this consciousness in a tormenting manner. Initially, he felt he was 'dislodged from the present', measured in the time of New York, Paris and London. That feeling turns into condemnation, which quickly turns into awareness, and then behaviour. Mexicans – like Arabs – had to embark on an adventure to discover time: the time of modernity.

Is modernity, Paz asks, an idea, a mirage or a moment of history? Regardless of the sometimes sharp theoretical debate and historiography of modernity, it is established that the Latin American – again, like that of the Arabs – quest for modernity through literature was part of the process of modernising their societies. And just as in the Arab world, modernisation became for Latin Americans a subject of ideological controversy and division.

Fully embracing modernity leads one back to one's roots through self-discovery. How exactly? The following quote by Paz explains this: 'Between tradition and modernity there is a bridge. When they are mutually isolated, tradition stagnates and modernity vaporises; when in conjunction, modernity breathes life into tradition, while the latter replies with depth and gravity.'

Paz's words wisely explained the dialectic of tradition and modernity framed by poetry and literature, but applicable to all aspects of life. This problem is identical to the one our own Arab culture experienced more than a century ago, and it continues to grapple with this alleged contradiction.

Arabs long thought that we in this world alone were concerned with this problem. Yet as we see, an author, intellectual and diplomat from Mexico followed modernity all the way to the source, with a sharp awareness that 'History's sun is the future'.

Since history is nothing but a series of constant changes, Paz declared that we 'adore change' as the prime engine of evolution in societies. And nothing underpins this change more than scientific and technological progress, which has profoundly altered the ideas that humanity had forged over many centuries.

However, this evolution created serious contradictions, some of which have come to threaten our species with extinction either because of scarce natural resources and the damage inflicted on the environment or because of the awesome power of destruction and devastation created by technology such as nuclear weapons.

Technological progress in the twentieth century was accompanied by two devastating world wars, along with tyranny, genocide, torture and oppression.

In the lecture he gave in 1990 against the backdrop of the collapse of the Socialist bloc, Octavio Paz questioned all philosophical and historical theories that called for human emancipation but that ended up building, as he put it, 'giant prisons'.

Yet the triumph of the free market economy, according to Paz, led to the prosperity of the few in an 'ocean of universal misery'. This economic model is linked to environmental degradation, and it pollutes souls just as it pollutes water, air and forests, and triggers a frantic race for production and consumption. It is an age of goods and waste: 'no other society has produced so much waste as ours has, material and moral'.

This diagnosis of the state of humanity today, which comes from experts of tortured human souls and the layers of being, reveals as well as the uniformity of human ordeals the uniformity of the possible solutions despite all difficulties. The modern and post-modern world have caused deep wounds in parallel with their amazing creations.

Once again, culture concerns all of us to tell our shared story and make new hopes and dreams, ones that are more accommodating of cultural diversity based on truth. The citizens of the world must be rescued from disillusionment through universal fraternity among people. This would not be impossible for those who created humanity's civilisation.

I recall here the words of the noble Quran: 'O mankind! We created you from a single (pair) of a male and a female, and made you into nations and tribes, that ye may know each other.'[8]

The readers should understand by now what I meant when I said that I had discovered literature was serious. I would add here that literature is vital for man's humanity.

## Cities and culture

In the context of the aesthetic discovery of the world, I want to address something that initially I had not paid any attention to, but as I edited this text it occurred to me in very clear terms.

Fate ordained that I would live in major cultural capitals, whether in the Arab world or outside it.

First, I found myself in Cairo. Cairo is a charming city that has been, it is no exaggeration to say, the beating heart of Arab culture since Arabs started being influenced by modernity.

Culture in Cairo experienced profoundly the dialectic of tradition versus modernity, revealing the heavy burden of inherited thinking and the extent and power of new ambitions and ideas. This emerged in Cairene arts, writing and theories.

I was also fond of the patriotic spirit that prompted our Egyptian brethren to declare that their country is *Umm al-Dunya*, Mother of the World. I did not see this as an isolationist, chauvinistic tendency so much as an expression of pride in the truly exceptional quality of the country that any visitor to Egypt may experience. After all, Egypt is heir to two of the greatest civilisations in history: the civilisation of ancient Egypt and the Arab–Islamic civilisation.

In fact, I owe Cairo much of the knowledge and experiences that broadened my horizons during my university years. Even if Cairo had only given me my wife Zainab, the woman with whom I have shared my life, seen good times and bad, and who has helped lighten the burdens of life and taken from me the task of raising my children, it would have been more than enough.

The path of my life produced a peculiar family and gave me the most blissful gift a man could hope for. I was born in Qatar, Zainab, my wife, is from Egypt, and my daughter, Iman, was born in Lebanon. My elder son, Tamim, was born in Syria and the younger, Imran, in France. And five of my ten grandchildren were born in the United States. The West, the East and the Gulf met under one roof, our original citizenships and our global citizenship coexisting in harmony.

The second foreign city I lived in was Beirut, and I drank from the sweet water of its culture. Beirut is the shape of the soul in the mirror, as Mahmoud Darwish, infatuated with the city, like many other great Arab poets, described it.

Beirut is a translucent city, pure like a polished mirror. It reveals different ideas and welds them together using a secret formula that only she knows. Everyone who lives in its bustling and often conflicting atmosphere, with its many moods and orientations, will soon feel as if he were born there.

The Lebanese capital has a strange power to expel feelings of alienation, and to embrace and even adopt its visitors. This is nothing unusual; the city is a melting pot, host to communities from different and diverse backgrounds.

Thanks to this, Beirut has produced a rich and pioneering brand of Arab culture, combining the Lebanese people's inherited openness from their adventurous seafaring ancestors with their sharp business acumen. Beirut remains the capital of Arab publishing, and a hub for engaging with other cultures, and I would almost say it has taught me *l'art de vivre* (the art of living).

The third Arab city I lived in and whose charm and magic I explored was Damascus. The streets of the Syrian capital are redolent with glory and history, and the city is home to many of the architectural edifices of the Umayyad Caliphate, of which it was also the capital.

There is a link between the city's long-standing history and architecture and its cultural and intellectual movements. Damascus, or the Jasmine Capital as it is known, was a meeting place for writers, artists and intellectuals when I served as Qatar's ambassador to Syria. Its intellectual and cultural salons echoed cultural movements from around the world, and students from every corner of the Arab world enrolled in its universities.

Damascus at the time was also the capital and altar of the Arabic language, whose purity it helped preserve all while contributing to its development to render it fit for the modern age. We also cannot speak about Arabic literature without mentioning its Syrian luminaries, early ones and contemporary, such as Khalil Mardam Beik, George Saidah, Shafiq Jabri, Nizar Qabbani, Fares Zarzour, Zakaria Tamer, Ghada al-Samman and Mohammad al-Maghout. There are others too numerous to list here.

It is difficult to understand Damascus's spirit without becoming acquainted with the traditional Damascene house. On the outside, it is a masterpiece of architecture; on the inside, it is a bustling world that comes to life with art and aesthetics.

After Cairo, Beirut and Damascus, Paris revealed to me many of its cultural and intellectual secrets, and New York its enthralling charisma.

As I recall my memories from these great centres of culture, I remember what Derek Walcott, the Caribbean Nobel Prize winner in 1992, said in his lecture: 'A culture, as we all know, is made by its cities.' I learned this, like all other people, by experiencing it first hand and in my own way.

My friends often ask me which city is closest to my heart. I find it hard to answer this question and usually say that they are all like friends whom I met when our paths crossed. Each has its own flavour, character, culture and appeal. Each one extended its friendship and helped enrich me culturally and intellectually. And although friends are not all the same, they are all friends none the less, and it is their different personalities that make life fresh and exciting.

There is something in my experience with cities closely related to literature, though not quite literary in nature itself: visual arts in general and painting in particular. What is common to both literature and visual arts is the aesthetic discovery of the world.

The connection between them is delicate and was best captured by José Saramago when he spoke before the Swedish Academy. He said, 'Painting is nothing more than literature achieved with paintbrushes … the man who cannot write paints or draws, as if he were a child.'

I have spoken on many occasions about my passion for art, especially Arabic calligraphy. Arabic calligraphy highlights aspects of the genius and aesthetics of Islamic art, based on transcending shapes of living things, bringing a pure spiritual dimension to drawing in line with the ideas of monotheism and abstraction; while Persian and other miniatures contain human and animal shapes, they are two-dimensional and devoid of perspective.

It is a precious opportunity in life to be given the chance to work and live in two culturally rich capitals like Paris and New York. It was in those cities that I came to appreciate visual and other arts, and developed a fondness for museums and their treasures. My visits to two of the world's top museums, the Louvre and the Metropolitan Museum, home to masterpieces of painting and sculpture, contributed greatly to my aesthetic exploration of the world.

Though I highlight the Louvre in Paris and the Metropolitan in New York, this does not mean that there are no equally important institutions elsewhere, such as the Hermitage in St Petersburg, the British Museum in London, and the many museums in Italy, particularly Florence. This is not to forget the National Museum in Berlin, the Prado in Madrid and the Rijksmuseum in Amsterdam. There are many breathtaking museums in Middle Eastern and North African countries as well, especially Cairo's Egyptian Museum, the Bardo National Museum in Tunisia, which houses a great collection of mosaics, and the museums of Syria, Iraq, Morocco, Algeria, Libya, Jordan and Lebanon.

My choice of the Metropolitan and the Louvre is a personal one, and has a lot to do with my postings to the two cities.

## The Louvre

My time in Paris (1979–84) allowed me to visit its many museums and closely follow art movements and cultural events. I was particularly fond of the Louvre, which I visited frequently, although there are many other museums and galleries in Paris which display all types of artworks.[9]

'The exceptional is accessible to all,' said Jean-Luc Martinez, president of the Louvre, describing the museum on its website. Martinez was saying that the extraordinary artworks on display at the museum are available for the public to enjoy freely, and also recalling that the time when high art was the preserve of the elite is gone. The Louvre is indeed an heir of the Enlightenment and the French Revolution, and is known as the 'museum of museums' for having inspired thousands of other museums around the world.

The Louvre is located in a building that as far back as the twelfth century was a royal palace and a residence for the kings of France. It is full of the most wonderful artistic creations from all cultures and all eras, and a cross section of various art schools and movements.

## The Metropolitan Museum

After Paris, my next posting was New York, where I served from 1984 until 1990. I lived in a bustling residential area between Fifth Avenue and Madison Avenue.

Madison Avenue is known for its galleries and exhibitions, displaying artworks from all around the world. One of my daily habits was, and still is, taking long walks, and Madison Avenue was one of the streets that I explored at length, often pausing in front of exhibition halls and checking the art on display.

The Metropolitan Museum of Art in New York is one of the world's greatest museums, housing treasures from the civilisations of both the ancient and modern worlds. I was particularly interested in the ancient Egyptian art and Islamic art collections, visiting them many times and spending hours contemplating the artistic relics of a glorious past. My apartment in New York was less than half an hour on foot from the Metropolitan and my family and I took full advantage of being so close to the museum to frequently visit its premises and its various exhibits, permanent and temporary.

The Metropolitan's story is the story of an exceptional American way of thinking, having been founded by private individuals and major donors. In the first page of the museum's guide, its director, Thomas Campbell, reminds us of the idea behind the museum's creation: 'Before the Metropolitan Museum owned a single work of art, it was an idea: a basic social and moral premise that access to art would fundamentally elevate anyone who encountered it. Individual thought would be heightened, industry and manufacturing would advance, a greater good would be achieved.'[10]

It is important to pay attention to these implicit principles in the introduction of a book celebrating the rich collection of the Metropolitan. It is astounding that what was literally nothing became a mere half-century later what we may call the largest encyclopaedic art museum in the world.

> *The concept of the encyclopedic or 'universal' museum stems from European models established during the Enlightenment. At the Met, our mandate is to collect the greatest artistic achievements of humankind, spanning all cultures and time periods, including objects that date back as far as the eighth millennium BC. These collections are highlighted in both the permanent installations devoted to each of our seventeen curatorial departments and the temporary exhibitions that focus on specific themes, time periods, or artists. Having this range of material within one museum creates an extraordinary dialogue between seemingly disparate histories and traditions and allows our visitors to literally traverse the globe in a single visit.*
>
> *In many ways, the Met's story is uniquely American. It is a tale of ambition, civic responsibility and profound generosity: an idea over lunch – 4 July 1866, in Paris – forged in the shadow of European museums that were defined by centuries of royal patronage. On that day, prominent American lawyer John Jay declared that the United States needed an art museum of its own. A group of fellow Americans in attendance pledged themselves to that goal, and the Metropolitan Museum of Art became a reality four years later.*
>
> *At the 1880 opening of its building in Central Park, the Met was heralded by Trustee Joseph C. Choate as in the 'vital and practical interest of the working millions.'[11]*

# The roles museums play

Visiting museums is a source of rich knowledge and a powerful incentive for cultivation and engagement with other cultures. Museums have their own terminology to be learned by frequenting them. Art has schools and each school has its pioneers, language, styles and masters whose lives and works cannot be properly understood without careful study. In part, this is why I devoted a lot of my time to museums and the arts in general.

As with all enriching sciences, visiting museums provided me with a solid background that made my work easier when I was entrusted with the cultural affairs of my country. It is my firm conviction that among the most important activities parents can undertake with their children is visiting museums regularly. They are second schools that open up children's minds, hone their talents and entice them to learn more.

In my opinion, nations secure their positions and instil confidence among their citizens about their present and their future by building and promoting museums. In a way, these are places to explore the past and its treasures, highlight the present and its arts, and incentivise people to work for a better future, by bringing together tradition and modernity. For this reason, it has been fortunate that Qatar has paid attention to museums and devoted huge resources to their development.

In this respect, I have much praise for the role of Sheikha Mayassa bint Hamad Al Thani in the world of arts and culture, and for her tremendous efforts in the area of museums. Sheikha Mayassa, who is Chairperson of the Board of Trustees of Qatar Museums, has certain qualities – notably her expertise in museums, arts and culture – that have made her the ideal person to take charge of this mission.

This has allowed her to play a key role in collecting art. Having worked directly with Sheikha Mayassa, I witnessed her dedication to this grand cultural undertaking, to say nothing of her refined taste, her appreciation for art and her faith in the part it plays. She closely follows the arts scene and has a personal desire for culture to take its rightful place in Qatar as a pillar of sustainable development. I also have nothing but praise for her administrative skills that I experienced firsthand, and her diligence, which has had a profound impact on her work and achievements.

## The Museum of Islamic Art

The small channel and the row of palm trees lining the path leading to the entrance of the Museum of Islamic Art reveal little about the marvellous treasures of Islamic creation waiting for one inside. The art works come from all three continents of the Old World, housed under the same roof in Doha. In creating the Museum of Islamic Art, Qatar wanted to construct a home for these works of art, in a building designed with no less splendour than its contents.

Between Central Asia, Persia and Andalusia, there are wide geographical expanses that the early Muslims traversed and populated and where they established civilisations, many of whose relics now sit in the Museum of Islamic Art. It is the first of its kind in the Gulf and is now one of the distinguished landmarks of Islamic museums around the world.

The museum houses masterpieces of Islamic art, including metalwork, ceramics, jewellery, woodwork, textiles and glass, collected from three continents and dating from the seventh to the nineteenth century.

The artworks are drawn from the treasure houses of princes to the personal homes of ordinary people. Each object tells a fascinating story about itself and the world it comes from.

The museum was inaugurated on 28 November 2008 under the patronage of His Highness Sheikh Hamad bin Khalifa al-Thani, Emir of the State of Qatar at the time.

The museum was designed by I. M. Pei, who placed it on an artificial island connected to land via a bridge. I. M. Pei was nominated to Qatar by the Aga Khan.

Between Ibn Tulun Mosque in Cairo and Doha, I. M. Pei sought inspiration from the Mamluk mosque for the Doha museum. He says, 'My feeling is that Islamic architecture often comes to life in an explosion of decorative elements, in the courtyards of the Umayyad Mosque in Damascus, or the interior of the Dome of the Rock in Jerusalem.'[12]

## The Museum of Modern Art

The Museum of Modern Art is located in Education City in Doha, inside an old building that was originally a school. The museum is home to a large collection of modern and contemporary Arab art, with 8,000 works produced over the past century. The collection started with the artworks acquired by Sheikh Hassan bin Mohammed bin Ali al-Thani, and gradually grew over the next twenty-five years.

In addition to displaying its unique collection, the museum holds regular activities and events, including temporary exhibitions, lectures and workshops, and publishes educational material.

## The Qatar National Museum

Unlike with the Museum of Islamic Art, which was inspired by the architectural history of the Arab–Islamic civilisation, French architect Jean Nouvel found inspiration in geography and geology for his Qatar National Museum design. The museum's exterior is reminiscent of the blade-like petals of the sand or desert rose, a mineral formation of crystallised sand found in the briny layer just beneath the desert's surface. Desert roses usually occur close to salt basins, and their shape depends on the amount of moisture and evaporation between the sandy layers; they change colour depending on the minerals present. They are lighter when the concentration of salt is higher, and darker when it is lower.

The museum, which is currently under construction and is expected to open in 2016, comprises a ring of low-lying, interlocking desert rose pavilions, which encircle a large courtyard area and encompass 430,000 square feet of indoor space.

Jean Nouvel's desert-inspired design is admirable. The life of the Arabs has been intricately linked to the vast desert extending from the Atlantic Ocean to the Arabian Gulf. I am confident this museum will be a cultural landmark that will stand out for both its design and the items that will go on display, highlighting the history and culture of Qatar.

# Chapter Four
# From *Majlis* to New Media

## Public space: communicating for freedom

In January 2015, in Paris, I met Nicolas Bordas, author of *The Killer Idea*.[13] It was a pleasant meeting, and we talked about many issues related to the media, communication and art. I found the title of his book quite interesting, given the intriguing paradox it suggests.

A killer idea alludes to a creative idea. Examining the history of ideas and of how they spread from one culture to another by various means, it becomes clear how important their role has been in enriching cultural interaction and encouraging individual and collective creativity. Within the dialectic of destruction, construction, birth, death and resurrection emerges the dynamic relationship between killer ideas and ideas that bring alive the fire of knowledge, changing the world in a way that serves humanity and its eternal dream of progress and freedom.

The foundation of this interaction between individuals, groups and cultures is communication. For Nicolas Bordas, civilisation and culture can only emerge thanks to this communication, which creates what he terms 'communicative societies' that have existed in civilised communities since ancient times. The Greek Agora, from four centuries BC, was but one embodiment of this communicative society.

Modernisation and globalisation have created new communicative realities. It is no longer possible to separate citizens from non-citizens, and nationals from foreigners. We live in an era that Bordas calls 'post-society', in that we live in more than one world and more than one society at the same time.

Globalisation, Bordas argues, is a culturally communicative phenomenon as much as it is an economic one. This much is clear in something like the World Wide Web and the expanded society it created after globalisation broke barriers gradually, and erased, even if virtually, borders, transcending geography. The global network has created a new geography, and opened new doors for historical potential that could go in various directions.

I recall in this regard the abolition of censorship in Qatar in 1995. I remember at the time having noted in a statement to the BBC that the decision was both a legal consecration of the freedom of the press available in my country and a declaration of a new era. It was a principled civil choice despite the risks it carried, such as defamation, assault on sanctities and attacks on sisterly and friendly countries, particularly those of the Gulf Cooperation Council (GCC). In the end, we put our trust in journalists' self-restraint and their commitment to the ethics of their profession, while encouraging a copyright law and creativity and innovation.

The rationale behind the decision was that the winds of change in the world were blowing in the direction of freedom of information. No one could stop this trend for one simple and almost self-evident reason: Who possessed the absolute truth in a pluralistic world that entitled them to decide what is good and what is not good for people? Does the desire to innovate and create not start out initially as an alien and shunned concept, as history tells us, before it proves its worth? Who can tell what is a 'killer idea' and what is a 'creative idea', without dialogue, negotiation, analysis and validation? Who gives a censor his or her power other than the capacity bestowed upon them by the state? If for the sake of argument we accept censorship is worthwhile, who guarantees the censor will not deviate from his or her remit, just like many bureaucrats, and invent narrower restrictions and stronger taboos?

Naturally, the issue is not this absolute. Right and wrong are clear, but discerning them requires conducting a dialogue about ethics and agreeing international standards regarding the freedom of thought and expression. The strongest censorship in the positive sense is the kind of censorship based on self-restraint and commitment stemming from an individual's human and universal values.

With regard to deviations and breaches, and literally killer ideas, these may be countered by immunising individuals ethically and culturally through public but profound dialogue where ideas and opinions are fought with ideas and opinions. Those who pursue censorship lack self-confidence and fail to recognise that a communicative society is in reality a dialogue society. Censors do not believe in the foundations of democracy either, namely the freedom and independence of the individual, which are inseparable from his or her commitment to duties and respect for the law.

## The *majlis* as a communicative society

I want to talk about an important space where I learned the foundations of social and cultural communication, as a member of a society that has its characteristic way of raising children within a public space and teaching them peaceful methods of conflict resolution: the *majlis*, as we call it in the Gulf countries, or *diwaniya* especially in Kuwait. The *majlis* has been placed on the UNESCO Representative List of Intangible Cultural Heritage.[14]

The *majlis* is an open space that varies in size depending on the stature of its owner. People meet there frequently without invitation or permission. It is rare for a home in the Gulf not to have one.

The non-Gulf readers may be interested to know that in our heritage the *majlis* has many functions, including social, cultural and even political. News and events are reported and discussed at the *majlis*, which is also often a forum for reciting poetry. Thanks to this oral interaction, principles, values and traditions are communicated to the younger generations.

In addition, community leaders meet in the *majlis* to discuss issues of their community to find the best ways to serve the common good. It is like the Gulf version of the Agora if we take the term used by the ancient Greeks, or what the Romans called the Forum.

While the desert climate forced our ancestors to resort to a sort of covered public square to shelter from the extreme heat, the similarities between the functions of the *majlis* and its equivalents in other cultures confirm that dialogue is firmly rooted in Gulf societies. The *majlis* is our own public space in which we learn rational debate, the principles of peace and the amicable resolution of any differences that may arise.

The *majlis* is a comprehensive system linking our heritage and local culture to our modern and universal character, and our individuals to our communities. It is in the *majlis* that individuals develop their shared language, art and literature, learn certain conducts and social mores, and accept shared outlooks as expressed by popular poetry, proverbs, customs, traditions and beliefs. The inclusive culture within the *majlis* provides a model that accommodates people who then adopt it voluntarily and bequeath it from generation to generation.

There can be no doubt here of the strong connection between the *majlis* and the tribe, the social unit that determines the form of relations between individuals internally and with other tribes. The tribe is the cornerstone of governance and administration of public affairs, and, to paraphrase an Arab poet, functions like a guiding light on dark, moonless nights.

The *majlis* has thus come to play a political role in good standing. The best example is how the *diwaniyah* in Kuwait, especially during elections, becomes the equivalent of a 'town hall' for the exchange of ideas, views and programmes for electoral campaigns, that also hosts political debates.

The tribe's role is to emphasise values such as solidarity, fraternity and forethought when making decisions, and consultation, solicitation of opinions and prudence in comportment. The aim is to achieve a delicate balance between the interests of the individual and those of the group.

The link between the tribe and the *majlis* means they both form part of an integrated social system that ensures communication among individuals, builds bridges between generations, facilitates cultural exchange, promotes higher values and entertains people. In the *majlis*, we welcome guests both in the daytime and at night-time for conversation, social occasions, and to take social decisions, organise marriage contracts, resolve family and social disputes and foster a spirit of harmony in the community.

This strong social role is accompanied by basic educational roles to impart skills that include respect, hospitality and etiquette. Young people learn how to listen, accept different opinions and respect those who are experienced. Values such as brotherhood, friendship, honesty and loyalty are also taught and promoted. For this reason, one finds fathers very keen to take their children with them to the *majlis*.

The *majlis* is also a cultural club in the full sense of the expression. Poems are read at the *majlis*, and visitors learn there the skills of oration. The *majlis* is also a source of information that broadcasts news in a way that respects people's privacy without engaging in defamation and libel.

I confess that for me the *majlis* is also intimately associated with the rich flavour of Arabic coffee, typically made with cardamom and saffron. The association is not just a personal impression; the preparation and presentation of Arabic coffee too embodies a strong tradition and culture.

As minister of culture, I sought together with Gulf culture ministers to register Arabic coffee in the UNESCO Representative List of Intangible Cultural Heritage. Coffee, as I see it, is not just a beverage we sip as part of a social norm, but is also one of the ways we greet each other in the Arab-Islamic way. The greeting generates a feeling of safety and whets the appetite for serious debate and exchange of opinions in pursuit of a common realty and harmonious vision.

## Abolishing the Ministry of Information

I have visited many *majlis*, some attended by prominent businessmen, others by artists and writers. Yet the political *majlis*, attended by leaders of the community and the country, have a special status. The *majlis* that has had the greatest impact on my life as a diplomat and minister occurred one day in 1997.

That day, I had the honour, as minister of culture and information, of meeting the Emir of Qatar in a routine gathering at his *majlis*. At first, nothing suggested it would be any different from many other previous meetings with this leader, who was well aware of the stakes the country faced vis-à-vis the region and the global stage. He was aware of all that progress and development required, and keen for his country to be at the heart of global modernisation.

Though I was in charge of the Ministry of Information, deep in my heart I was not convinced of the usefulness of having a ministry for this important sector. To my mind, such ministries have no role other than restricting freedoms, imposing censorship and steering people in a single direction in contravention of freedom of opinion and expression.

I knew how humble the emir was with all ministers and citizens and was familiar with his intelligence, shrewdness and knowledge of successful economic and cultural models around the world. For this reason, I did not hesitate to approach him directly about what was preoccupying me.

The emir's reaction was to recall something that is almost obvious. 'In developed nations,' he said, 'there are no ministries of information. Any ministry of information is a chain restricting the freedom of expression and thought.' The emir quietly asked for more explanation and clarification, and I expounded in detail on the position of governments on the issue of freedoms in those countries that have come a long way in this regard.

I thought that the issue would be one of many mentioned casually in conversation like dozens of others in the *majlis*. Therefore, it came as a surprise when the emir asked me to prepare a careful and clear study about the issue, supported with evidence. Weeks later, I returned with the report. Without hesitation, when it became clear to the emir that this was the right thing to do, he issued a decree abolishing the Ministry of Information.

I thus became the first minister to eliminate his own job at his own suggestion. But it was an offering I gladly made at the altar of the freedom of expression. Were it not for Sheikh Hamad bin Khalifa al-Thani, the Father Emir of the State of Qatar, and his vision for profound modernisation, I would not have been successful in my quest to become the last Qatari minister of information.

In truth, I had worked as a journalist at one stage of my life, and I knew well what kind of pressures and strict restrictions Arab journalists have to contend with. For this reason, when I made my proposal, I had faith in the wise saying that lighting a candle is better than cursing the darkness.

## The Doha Centre for Media Freedom

The abolition of the ministry did not remove me from the world of media, however. The divorce between my duties as minister of information and me was not a divorce from the world of information, press and opinion. In fact, it was the beginning of a new phase that was different in content, context and process from the former one.

In this context, and together with Sheikh Hamad bin Thamer al-Thani, I founded the Doha Centre for Media Freedom in 2008. Our intention was to contribute as much as possible to supporting the freedom of the media in accordance with the Universal Declaration of Human Rights. The declaration guarantees the right of every person to freedom of opinion and expression – including the freedom to hold opinions without interference and to seek, receive and impart information and ideas through any media and regardless of frontiers.

Unfortunately, restrictions on information and the media, and on ideas and intellectuals, are very pronounced in the Arab world and in many other countries. This reminds me of an interview with al-Araby al-Jadeed in 2014, when I answered questions about intellectuals and the Arab Spring. The interviewer asked me what I thought about accusations that Arab intellectuals had failed to deal properly with the repercussions of the Arab Spring. Many of them ended up siding with tyrannical and authoritarian regimes, against the aspirations of their people. My answer was that this verdict was harsh and unfair.[15]

The Arab intellectual faces, in addition to restrictions from the authorities and the regional environment, radical changes in the structure of the media. In effect, there are many similarities between the satellite television boom in the last two decades of the twentieth century and the information revolution in the twenty-first century. Both have had a profound impact on the official Arab media landscape, which the Arab Human Development Report has since 2003 described as authoritarian and unilateral.

In my 2005 book, I argued that the official media is often authoritarian, 'where the authorities invade the media discourse, and set its agenda, directions, values, and even details, choices, and scheduling' and that its entire resources are 'devoted to cover the activities, meetings, and pompous statements of officials'. It is also unilateral, 'where the discourse often excludes the other and prevents it from appearing before the public opinion', and is state-controlled, with 'the majority of Arab media outlets confused vis-à-vis some or most developing political events pending instructions or ignore important events'.[16]

However, there was one bright spot in the Arab media landscape at that time. 'The good news is that these phenomena are eroding, not purposefully but thanks to developments that have imposed themselves on officials, including such developments as the satellite channels.' We can update what I said back then by substituting 'new media' for 'satellite channels'.

I still believe that the 'impact of these channels did not stop at the main element of the communicative process, namely the audience, but went beyond to rearrange the agendas of other media outlets, be they Arab or Western, or print, broadcast, or electronic media, and also imposed themselves on decision-making circles and the agendas of Arab citizens'.

## The New Media Revolution: The question of the elite and the general public

In his book *The New Media*,[17] Sadok Hammami examines the very foundations of the media and the relationship between broadcaster and receiver in an analysis that is both spot on and profound. The issues he addresses are at the heart of our overview cultural diplomacy, the media and the new media.

No doubt what is known as Web 2.0 has turned upside down the hierarchy built upon the binary of a specialised elite producing information and manipulating meaning and the general public, whose role is strictly to receive the message and the information. The question that accompanied the Internet revolution was simple but profound: 'Are we witnessing today the decline of the intellectual and of power?'[18]

Behind this burning question is a sense of the major transformation humanity is going through, a transformation that has brought the authority of the intellectual into question. It also – implicitly – highlights a model that has been at the heart of the media since the emergence of the press, a model that is in many ways elitist and authoritarian.

My opinion is that the foundation of traditional media outlets, including print media, radio and television, was built on the separation of broadcaster and receiver. The mode of participation in the public sphere in the media and in the production of public discourse was limited to passive consumption. These were areas monopolised by the political, cultural and media elites, based on what they perceived as their legitimate representation of the whole of society.

This explains, by the same logic, why some intellectuals, journalists and politicians claim to speak on behalf of 'silent individuals and communities', thanks to their command of the language, knowledge and instruments of discourse, argument and ideational production. The elite believe from this perspective that they are the vanguard of social awareness and that they alone can express it.

By contrast, the audience becomes a nebulous entity in this outlook, the audience being the entity targeted by the elite through broadcast media messages.

The notion of 'popular culture' was devised with latent pejorative connotations, to draw a distinction between a knowledgeable culture and a non-knowledgeable culture, each with its own sets of rules and processes.

The term 'mass media', in turn, summarises the unilateral, vertical and authoritarian structure of traditional media, as the audience targeted by the media are readers, listeners and viewers.

One of the functions of the mass media from the prevailing perspective is to lift the public to a higher awareness and finer tastes, and to prevent the public from submitting to its whims so as not to fall into vulgarity and the culture of the rabble, proceeding from a purely consumerist foundation.

Interesting in this context is a position that may not resonate well with the public, which is adopted by prominent literary figures such as Joseph Brodsky. In his lecture on the day he received the Nobel Prize in Literature, he said:

> *Art in general, literature especially, and poetry in particular, is not exactly favoured by the champions of the common good, masters of the masses, heralds of historical necessity … Nowadays, there exists a rather widely held view, postulating that in his work a writer, in particular a poet, should make use of the language of the street, the language of the crowd. For all its democratic appearance, and its palpable advantages for a writer, this assertion is quite absurd and represents an attempt to subordinate art, in this case, literature, to history. It is only if we have resolved that it is time for Homo sapiens to come to a halt in his development that literature should speak the language of the people. Otherwise, it is the people who should speak the language of literature.*

What is required, in my view, is a two-way process that satisfies all sides. Elevating discourse, language and substance is a continuous but feasible endeavour as proven by authors in all languages. At the same time, the receivers must not be treated with condescension, as this could create in them an aversion to the creative world and produce a schism between the content creator and the receiver.

By analogy with the language of creativity and its finesse, the language of the media should strive to achieve a delicate balance between seeking to refine the tastes of the public and its awareness and the clarity and delivery of the discourse.

Prestige, knowledge and humility are in the end very compatible notions.

The public in undemocratic communities is like a black hole into which media content and messages collapse without making so much as an echo. The public consumes and then falls silent, or, to use a French saying from the 1970s, it is asked to 'be beautiful and shut up!' But public opinion in democratic communities is the antithesis of authority, expressing individuals' opinions in a dynamic way. Political elites fear public opinion, and spare no means to study it and analyse it with a view to pre-empting its trends, predicting its directions and, naturally, influencing it.

As we mentioned earlier, the vertical relationship between the broadcaster and the receiver is in the process of changing as a result of the revolution in the media. The public itself now produces content, thanks to the new media, particularly social media. During the Arab Spring, social media would prove its worth as a means of expression, mobilisation, organisation and communication among large numbers of users.

Figures in the Gulf nations, for example, show that there are more than twenty-two million users out of 50.7 million people (2014). Data from the Qatari Ministry of Telecommunications, the Ministry of Development Planning and Statistics, the International Monetary Fund and the World Economic Forum indicate that the proportion of Internet users in Qatar is 98 per cent, with Qatar ranking twenty-third out of 137 countries on the Internet readiness index.

A high percentage are Facebook users (1.32 million out of 2.2 million people), and Twitter users are thought to number around 112,000. It is worth noting that almost half of Facebook users are aged nineteen to twenty-nine. The main activities on social media in Qatar are, in order of importance, chatting, sharing information, expressing opinions and file sharing.

Régis Debray, a French philosopher and media expert, presents a sober analysis of the relationship between culture and media, and lays the foundations for 'Mediology'[19] by emphasising the 'technological transfer of cultural forms'. Debray believes there are three technical and social mediums that have governed human cultural history: a rhetorical medium based on oral communication, followed by a written medium based on writing, and then an audiovisual medium in which the audiovisual media became the dominant form of communication.

Sadok Hammami, echoing this view, argues that the dominant discourse considers the new media to mark a break with traditional media in terms of the technology used, the models that govern it and the content it produces. New media is a domain in which innovative media forms and communicative practices are emerging in a way hitherto unknown to humankind. Examples include the electronic press, citizen journalism, social media, blogs and so on.

In light of Debray and Hammami's analyses, we can raise questions about whether the new media now constitutes a fourth medium, where the interlocutors differ from the three previous ones in that, and perhaps for the first time, they consist of the audience itself. The audience now produces content and meaning, rather than the traditional elite which has hitherto monopolised this function and its mediums.

In the past I wrote the following:

> Developments in the media accelerated the circulation of information and ideas across newspapers, radios, satellite channels and the internet, causing major tremors in the Arab world. This became a source of concern among the ruling regimes. Perhaps the problem is that some Arab media outlets got out of the control of governments, as Arab government-owned media … appeared impotent next to media outlets that now had influence going beyond the usual scope.
>
> The outlets in question soon became a breathing space for the often-excluded citizens, and ordinary readers and viewers now had a visible presence on their pages and programmes. This development provided an opportunity for thinkers, writers and opinion makers who were too much for the official

*media to bear to present their views and ideas without patronisation or pres-*
*sure, though there have been intruders here and there.*

*The explanation for this is that the new type of media started revealing*
*previously unknown aspects. The new media spoke in a language that was*
*absent before, leading to a decline in the influence of the traditional annoying*
*sycophantic discourse.*[20]

In this context, we cannot overlook a unique media phenomenon that has had a profound impact throughout the Arab world and beyond, meaning Qatar's Al-Jazeera. Al-Jazeera emerged in the last decade of the twentieth century, breaching a stagnant and degraded media scene dominated by sycophancy and glorification of leaders, as we mentioned earlier.

Whether one agrees with its editorial line or not, Al-Jazeera caused a ripple in the stagnant waters of the Arab media, attracting tens of millions of viewers thirsty for different approaches to news coverage. Al-Jazeera was also the incentive and model for other satellite channels, such as Al-Arabiya, France 24 and Sky News.

## On public television: issues and wagers

Public television has a vital political, economic, social and cultural function. Perhaps for this reason, the overwhelming private ownership of satellite channels, in contrast to the state domination of television in previous decades, has not meant that public television has been abandoned.

Public television has remained a public service unbound by market logic guaranteeing political and intellectual diversity as a reflection of the social mosaic. Public television is also supposed to offer educational, social and cultural services (including audiovisual productions) that privately owned televisions do not produce because of their limited commercial viability. Thus, taxpayers fund public television channels such as France's TF1, Britain's BBC and Germany's Deutsche Welle.

The breathtaking development of modern communication, however, raises questions about the function of public television in the context of new media. Is the Internet an additional means for public television to use to introduce its function as a public service? Or will the Internet open new doors and other functions for public television, such as sharing, interaction and continuous regeneration, to keep pace with the constantly changing political, economic, cultural and social contexts?

While public television, with its historic precedence and links to the state, is a totem of traditional media, it also represents a cultural institution with diverse social functions, in addition to its political functions. However, the fundamental shift occurred with the advent of privately owned radio stations and television channels, as capital and commercial conglomerates launched investments in the media world.

Naturally, private interests have different goals and strategies centred on profit. There is no dispute about how far private media has come in technology and aesthetics, and in launching initiatives and discovering interesting and entertaining ideas in the media and publicity market, driven in part by fierce competition. As a result, the focus shifted from social and cultural functions to entertainment and even sensationalism to attract viewers and listeners.

This has meant that the ethics of journalism, however, had to accommodate publicity and marketing techniques. Many problems emerged because of this, including selecting news that will quickly resonate with public opinion at the expense of the principles and ethics of the profession. Further complicating matters is the link between the interests of capitalists and business conglomerates and the political aspirations and roles that the media can help fulfil.

The need for public media remains because of the growing role of the private sector in the media globally, the tendency of capital to monopolise, the risk of political exploitation and cultural stereotyping, and the overemphasis on entertainment. Public media can be an equalising force within the audiovisual scene in each country towards reinforcing the ethics of journalism in selecting and drafting news. Public media can give a platform to various views, moderate public debate and preserve the media's cultural and social role by being a public service funded by the taxpayer.

True democracy is after all based on securing the freedom of expression, where citizens have the right to access information and participate in the media. The private media, however, with its commercial goals and its focus on advertisement revenues, has little interest in these lofty ideals.

Let us not be fooled by the boom in private satellite channels in the Arab world, in line with the trend globally. Public media, I believe, remains crucial to building a balanced and pluralistic society. Public media is a safety valve for the community and for those who do not have enough capital to communicate their views. Public media is a boon for citizenship based on the freedom of the individual and participation in opinion and decision-making in relation to public affairs.

I want to discuss some other trends in our world today, even if the Arab media has yet to pick these up. But the butterfly effect could soon change this.

Many broadcasters today focus on local affairs in regions, cities and even individual neighbourhoods. This is worthwhile if only because it fulfils the proximity criterion of media coverage, where journalists are closer to the source of the news and the preoccupations of the citizenry. A sort of Agora is created this way, reinforcing the sense of citizenship.

In parallel, there is a trend towards specialised media, with outlets focusing on business, sports, tourism, women or music, and even specific genres of music such as jazz. Again, this is worthwhile because it responds to the diversity of tastes and needs, and because these outlets offer in-depth, targeted content.

These two trends strike a balance between the mass nature of media outlets by addressing a general audience, and the individualistic, independent and diverse nature of democratic societies.

Despite these trends, I still believe public media outlets with a comprehensive scope are an absolute necessity, not only because of the aforementioned functions but also because of these trends geared towards specialisation and targeted audiences. Comprehensive media serves as a link among individuals and communities no matter how different they may be.

The comprehensive public media goes beyond the local, regardless of the importance of a targeted coverage of local affairs. It also rescues specialisation from the danger of having a partial and incomplete approach. By achieving these two aims, the comprehensive public media fulfils the function of collective cooperation and helps build a common identity.

Communication and dialogue among individuals and communities, and granting them all the right to express themselves in the media and partake in developing ideas, is a guarantor of citizenship and national identity. The role of the media in building, protecting and enriching national identity is no less important than that of the school, which makes it a social service just like healthcare and education.

## Art television: The first meeting available to all

I would like to point out some important pioneering examples of specialised media. I mention one that I see as a model of the media that can complement public media and go a long way towards making culture accessible to everyone, and contribute in one way or another to building peace in the minds, hearts and eyes of people.

Until the end of the nineteenth century, fine music was available exclusively in theatres and at the opera, which were accessible only to the elite. It was not possible to access and enjoy music except in these luxurious venues.

The radio was therefore a genuine revolution in this regard, disseminating music throughout the world. Simple farmers, workers and housewives were now able to learn about and enjoy music. This is how the West came to know Arab and African music, and vice versa, and the same goes for all other continents and regions.

But this revolution did not come in visual arts, as Elizabeth Markevitch, director of ikono, notes.[21] Most major artworks are parked in museums or made available through exhibitions, and it is hard to ensure that everyone visits these. It is difficult for someone from an African nation to visit the Met in New York, or someone from Latin America to visit the Louvre in Paris.

The enjoyment of major works of art is a luxury denied to most people around the world. This was the thinking behind the idea of a dedicated television channel that features art from all over the world, from prehistoric cave paintings found at Lascaux right up to modern architecture.

Ikono's very succinct slogan is 'We let art talk'. No text, comments or audio accompany the images, allowing everyone, no matter who they are, to enjoy that first look at a work of art. After that, they can either content themselves with that first contact or deepen their knowledge if they wish.

When she speaks of the first meeting with art, Elizabeth Markevitch alludes to the meaning intended by French writer André Malraux when he wrote about the first encounter between the eye and a work of art. We may look away and move on, we may become curious and draw closer, or we may be enthralled at first sight and feel a strong attraction we do not fully understand.

Our first contact with a painting, for example, is a glance. The eye makes a physical and emotional contact. Afterwards, we may stop and think about the art, and check what critics and art experts wrote and so on. But the first glance is the raw experience that connects us to a given painting.

Ikono gives viewers the chance to have that experience with artworks, and for this alone it deserves our praise. Interestingly, Markevitch launched her project at the same time YouTube was emerging, in the middle of the first decade of the twenty-first century. There are many significant conclusions to be made regarding this concomitance, some of which we shall examine in the coming paragraphs.

## Citizen journalism: thus spoke the unknown individual

What we said about private versus public media, or comprehensive versus specialist media, is only a small part of the big picture that shows how complex modern societies and communication have become. The technological quantum leap has made this picture even more complex, and we specifically mean here the Internet and the phenomena it gave rise to, where sound, images and texts combine and interact.

These technologies caused ruptures in knowledge, and are worthy of attention in general despite reservations and caveats, especially in terms of their role in promoting communication between people and expanding individual and collective freedoms.

I share Sadok Hammami's view that the Internet fundamentally broke the strict separation between the elites and the masses. That separation existed not because of the nature of each entity or the barriers between them, as it might appear at first glance, but because of their roles and wagers.

Today, we see citizens themselves producing information, even if in raw form, and communicating their messages and ideas through their mobile phones or personal computers. Citizens are no longer passive receptors subservient to the power of professional newsmakers and commentators.

We are looking therefore at a new dynamism in producing and receiving information, thanks to simplified applications for content production, distribution and promotion. As a result, information can now be produced by a broad segment of the population.

If we carefully examine this historic rupture, we soon realise that the media's power, as understood as a hold on the means of producing content, has expanded and assimilated hitherto unknown individuals and the general public. For this reason, we should not be surprised that many bloggers have become stars in various societies or that thousands upon thousands of people follow certain names active on Twitter.

Prominent intellectuals, writers and media stars, who would otherwise be the masters of writing and journalism, had to set up blogs on the websites of their newspapers, presenting their opinions like all other 'citizen journalists'. They understood the decline of their power with the decline of print media, and realised that new formats such as blogging and micro-blogging resonate more with people. What they have done is to quickly put the brakes on their decline at the same time as they reserved a place for themselves in the digital media world, which brings to the fore the power of the citizen journalist, the hitherto unknown individual, to use Sadok Hammami's terms.

The amusing thing is that on blogs and Twitter feeds one can see the tweets and views of ordinary people and those of well-known commentators side by side. The media and cultural elite receded, both literally and metaphorically, against the tide of ordinary masses. They descended from their ivory towers to the streets or lost their old halo and their esoteric secrets. We must appreciate this development regardless of its implications, positive or negative.

None of this would have happened were it not for the ease with which the Internet makes it possible to create and manage websites and accounts on social media services and blogging sites, often free of charge. This is not to mention the interactive character that gives this medium its special appeal for writing, publishing, commenting and debating.

What happened is a radical break with the main brokers of information, namely journalists. These new formats for disseminating information turned any citizen with access to the Internet into a potential journalist.

But in my opinion, the issue goes further than this and touches upon the concept of power itself. The transformation in the media is a transfer and break-up of power.

As is known, the intellectual elite, particularly the media elites, were often allied to the political elite on the basis of shared interests. Sometimes this alliance, which took many forms, would be implicit. For example, politicians would give journalists scoops or interesting stories in return for favourable coverage. At other times, it would be explicit to the point where journalists openly glorified and adulated politicians.

This is common all over the world. Everyone knows of it yet everyone acquiesces to it, possibly because it has existed since the emergence of the media.

As with all other phenomena that emerge and grow without being analysed, people quickly develop perceptions that are hard to debunk later. Nevertheless, who today trusts official information sources when footage filmed by ordinary people often exposes a different and contradictory angle to the official account?

Examples of these videos uploaded by ordinary people on social media are too numerous to count. Media outlets, both official and private, now themselves rely on such footage in covering events that professional reporters cannot access. Some of the greatest scoops of today come from ordinary people armed with nothing more than a smartphone.

Either way, images and videos are more trustworthy than news bulletins. The value of images online is plain for all to see, especially on services like Instagram.

I had had the impression that my long career as an ambassador and then minister meant that people knew about me what anyone should know about any public figure in diplomacy and culture. But my impression completely changed when I started using Instagram to communicate with people. From their comments and responses, it seemed as though they were becoming acquainted with me for the first time, asking for more news, information and events. I have since become an active user of Instagram.

Society is evolving relentlessly. Even if one is well known to one generation, he may be unknown to the next. However, social media helps in keeping us up to date, and in renewing information and attitudes.

I noticed this through my experience on Instagram, especially in a country where young people make up a large proportion of the population. However, my experience on Instagram was not limited to Qatar, as I have communicated with people in the Arab world and beyond.

I now have to constantly communicate with people, and post memories, events and views. I admit I feel pleased with this intellectual and cultural exchange, and eagerly await responses to the thoughts I share as a diplomat or an intellectual. A rich and enjoyable exchange has ensued between my followers and me.

Instagram has motivated me to publish many observations related to my intellectual journey, some of which were not very well known. Instagram also allowed me to document events and introduce figures I met from various political, cultural and intellectual backgrounds as part of a series I called 'Men time has graced us with'.[22]

The reactions of my followers made me appreciate people's interest in what I post. I felt it was their right to learn about events related to me personally and my career, which is perhaps one of the key motivations behind this book.

## The shifts in the media and the crisis of democracy

The deep transformations in the media and new media are inseparable from other profound transformations in societies and cultures, and from the crisis of democracy itself. By this, I mean representative democracy at a time when society is strongly veering towards a more participatory mode of democracy. Citizens who have lost confidence in traditional politics no longer readily buy into the elites' merchandise.

Making matters worse, the wager by political, economic and media elites on excessive domination and their suspicious bravado led to manipulation of voters and the public, often using marketing techniques. Although this achieved some provisional results for them, they ultimately shook faith in politics as the best way to govern.

It is not a coincidence, therefore, that there has been growing interest, even at the heart of national institutions, in issues such as good governance, transparency, accountability and political participation. All this in my view is a result of the interaction between the political class and civil society, and it tends to create an equilibrium between various branches of power, particularly by reinforcing the critical 'fourth estate'. The outcome is a shift in general culture and political culture in particular, as monopoly is eroded politically, economically and culturally, and the sharp separation between the elite and the masses is overcome.

By the same token, many notions proposed by Marxism, which for long monopolised social criticism, collapsed. I return to the valuable work of Sadok Hammami, who argues that concepts like 'revolutionary intellectuals', 'avant-garde intellectuals' and 'organic intellectuals' are obsolete, like many concepts that spread in our Arab culture in the 1960s and 1970s.[23] Because the intellectuals' old halo has been shattered, they no longer monopolise criticism and opinion and lose the privilege of having the absolute understanding of reality and the 'false awareness' of the masses.

The source of the intellectual's former power was access to information. But today, since information is available to everyone, what will be the intellectual's fate? Can the intellectual preserve his or her old role with the evolution of popular and mass culture, in form, content and format?

Popular culture has proven, even before the revolution in information and communication technology, that the masses of ordinary people can assimilate social norms, develop their own standards and ethics and adapt and coexist smoothly. The digital revolution reinforced popular culture, expanding people's horizons. A deeper impact should be expected going forward, the simple rule being that ideas in a process of interactive reception will continue to modulate both their content and potency to take into account feedback.

The horizontal relationship allowed by information and communication technology in my belief is built on the ruins of the vertical relationship between the elite and the masses. This has not only altered the starting point for news coverage and commentary, but also reinvigorated the analytical abilities of individuals in relation to content and context.

Clearly, the source of this proactive reception, so to speak, is what distinguishes the Internet. The interactive character prevents the domination of a single ideology or view.

Yet this does not mean we should be unmindful of the many risks accompanying post-information revolution trends. Many of them are moral hazards, including those that affect human rights such as trafficking of women and children, and the dissemination of false or misleading information. This is not to mention security risks related to organised crime, cybercrime and terrorism.

## Doors of freedom

The revolution in social media has had tremendous influence, both negative and positive, not just on ideas but on people's lives. In the Arab Gulf region, which is affluent and technologically advanced, there have been huge risks because the pace of social media evolution follows a steeper curve than intellectual, educational and social development.

Social media is often used to pass on a variety of messages and reinforce certain notions and directions, sometimes without the receiver being aware of them. In this way, social media can be a source of grave danger for those without the critical faculties needed to distinguish good from bad.

People with certain agendas can thus exploit social media. Some in the audience, many of whom lack the factual knowledge to put things in perspective, are influenced and proceed to promote these agendas, out of a genuine enthusiasm for certain stances, as they find themselves hostage to these convictions. Others, while not lacking in knowledge, may lack a sense of responsibility.

Yet it is naïve to think that opening the doors of freedom will not cause tremors and let through fears and risks. It would be more worthwhile to keep pace with people's new visions and ideas, which are likely to expand the horizon of freedom and bring people and nations closer together. Freedom and its potential hazards are no doubt much better than tyranny, which denies people their humanity and fundamental freedoms as expression, thought and open communication.

# Chapter Five
# On Cultural Diplomacy

## Addressing hearts and addressing minds

When, at a meeting of the ministers of culture of the Gulf Cooperation Council, I called for a cultural festival to be held in tandem with Gulf summits, it was not my intention to add yet another event to the busy cultural and intellectual calendars of these countries. Already, many Gulf capitals are international hubs for visual arts and cinema, having proved their cultural and artistic development and their openness to world cultures, as well as their overwhelming desire to become acquainted with and engage with other cultures.

In my country, we consciously choose cultural exchange as a major component of our cultural strategy. We are an open country by necessity and by virtue of the multiculturalism of the expatriates working in Qatar. We hope to be a model in our diverse world, where human differences are managed on an ethical and humane basis for the sake of peace and coexistence among people.

At the Qatari Ministry of Culture, Arts and Heritage, we launched a translation series to function as a bridge between Arab culture and the ideas crystallising around the world, regarding issues of shared concern. We also developed a plan to celebrate each year a culture from a selected country, such as the United Kingdom, Brazil, Japan and Turkey. This event has had encouraging results in the context of bilateral cultural diplomacy, both politically and economically, not to mention the mutual knowledge and understanding it creates so that the tree of peace between people may grow and bloom.

But my proposal to my GCC colleagues was intended to establish a common space that highlights the cultural and human values in our Gulf countries, a space where local traditions can interact as tributaries that enrich the great river of Arab and human culture beyond it. The proposal we made on behalf of the State of Qatar is built on a profound belief that culture is the melting pot for noble values – local, national and global – to combine in a way that strengthens citizenship in all its aspects.

While the cultural unity of the GCC countries is well established, and corroborated by the similarities of their cultures and the uniformity of their language, religion and traditions, the confluence of cultural actors from the peoples of these countries would be an occasion to reinforce this bond and link it to the Arab culture, the global culture and the new values that humanity continues to adopt.

In reality, the proposal comes from a firm belief, evident in the cultural history of human relations, that culture bring peoples and nations closer together. A paradox here is that separate identities and local traditions emerge most in the cultural realm. However, at the same time, it is the realm where various modes of expression, diverse art forms and human values can converge, as these are the best embodiment of the relationship between individuals and groups, and existence and fate.

I have long believed that attention to culture would be a source of power for the desired Gulf political entity currently embodied by the GCC, and an ideal formula to invest in Gulf citizens beyond the 'oil and gas human' stereotype and towards the ambitious, life-affirming human who dreams of a better world based on peace and solidarity.

This proposal falls between multilateral cultural diplomacy and the collective diplomacy imposed by regional blocs. In both cases, the essence and the goal are one and the same: building human capacity through culture and integrating culture in human development, as well as seeking understanding among peoples to build a culture of peace.

The concept of soft power may perhaps clarify my vision for cultural diplomacy and my proposal for a GCC cultural event to accompany GCC summits.

## Arab World Institute and soft power

The concept of soft power ushered in a new stage of so-called cultural diplomacy in the world, its key idea being to use culture to influence hearts and minds. The aim behind cultural diplomacy is to prepare a cultural and psychological climate that is consistent in lifestyle and thinking. Indeed, the world is increasingly moving towards values such as democracy, freedom and human rights. Cultural diplomacy is a clever investment in the culture and human resources of another people in order to leave a profound mark on the minds and consciences of that people, who would in turn spread those shared values.

The path to the hearts is a culture of ideas, values and beliefs, and the only weapons are persuasion and influence. Ideas are the best and most lasting instruments, as they spread along paths that do not recognise red lines or barriers.

The target audience in cultural diplomacy is the citizens of other countries. They would be invited in different formats to adopt perceptions and values, and then share them. The Arab World Institute in Paris is possibly the best example of this.

When I served as Qatar's ambassador in Paris, the Council of Arab Ambassadors was comprised of many prominent, experienced, conscientious and forward looking ambassadors.[24] These ambassadors had a major interest in culture. We routinely discussed the best ways to introduce our Arab culture in one of the great capitals of art and intellect. The goal was for culture to play its role as an instrument of soft power to serve Arab–French relations.

The French governments during that period shared our vision. I was a contemporary of two presidents of the Fifth Republic, Valéry Giscard d'Estaing (1974–81) and François Mitterrand (1981–96). The foreign ministers under them were Jean François-Poncet (1978–81) and Claude Cheysson (1981–4) respectively. Both paid great attention to relations with the Arab world. Minister Cheysson set an important precedent that became the norm by holding a monthly meeting with Arab ambassadors at a famous café outside Paris on weekends. The discussions during those meetings were open and not subject to any agendas, and took place in a very cordial atmosphere, although urgent developments sometimes imposed themselves on the meetings.

I remember that our group of ambassadors was aware of the role of culture and its centrality in the dialogue between civilisations and nations. It was clear to us that others' ideas about the Arab world were marred by confusion and ambiguity. Thus, we started thinking of ways to introduce Arab culture in a serious manner, away from the short-term vagaries of politics.

The idea of the Arab World Institute came to light under Minister François-Poncet and started being implemented during the meetings with Minister Cheysson. The truth is that I feel very gratified about my modest role in proposing the idea, from the time it was a project until the time the Arab World Institute was established, becoming a staple reality of cultural life in Paris.

It is worth pointing out that President Giscard d'Estaing allocated a plot of land opposite the Hilton in the 15th arrondissement to be the home of the Arab World Institute in Paris. The Arab ambassadors were enthusiastic about this given the commercial importance of that location.

When his successor, President Mitterrand, a man highly interested in culture, took over, he felt that the plot of land was unsuitable. His view was that it was a commercial location while he considered the

Institute a purely cultural institution which should be located in the cultural heart of Paris, close to universities and cultural institutions in the 1st arrondissement.

I admit today that this upset some Arab ambassadors in the beginning. They wrongly believed that Mitterrand was undermining the Institute by keeping it away from a commercially significant location, and that the socialist government did not have the same enthusiasm for Arab–French relations as its predecessors.

Mitterrand made his decision and the land on which the Institute is located today was chosen. Jean Nouvel, as mentioned earlier one of France's foremost architects and the same architect who would later design the Qatar National Museum in Doha, was selected to design the Institute.

Over time, it became clear that Arab–French relations under Mitterrand remained excellent. The Socialist president's first visit abroad was to Saudi Arabia, a strong signal that he was keen to maintain the friendship.

And Mitterrand's choice turned out to be the right one. His decision to place the Institute in the cultural district of Paris was far-sighted. The Institute has become a beacon of Arab culture in one of the world's most important cultural capitals.

The Arab World Institute is today a cultural bridge between the Mashreq and Maghreb, and between the Arab world and the West, the fruit of a partnership between France and the majority of the Arab League member states. The Institute is governed by French law. It seeks to highlight the contributions of the Arab world to global civilisation and introduce it to French and European audiences, in addition to promoting dialogue between East and West.

According to its literature, the Arab World Institute in France aims to deepen studies and knowledge about the Arab world, its language, its culture and its development efforts. The Institute also seeks to support cultural exchange, communication and cooperation between France and most Arab countries, especially in science and technology. The Institute has helped develop profound relations between the Arab world and France, which also constitute a solid basis for strengthening relations with other European nations.

Upon its inauguration in 1987, the Arab World Institute became a distinctive space that blended smoothly into the cultural fabric of the French capital. The Institute is home to a museum of Arab and Islamic art, a special library and a lecture hall. Year after year, the Institute has successfully held a variety of events revolving around art, culture, literature, music, cinema, dance, architecture, photography and youth activities from the Arab world. The Institute opens its doors to discussions, dialogue and intellectual exchanges through seminars and lectures, and publishes *Qantara*, a quarterly magazine.

The Arab World Institute offers a comprehensive programme for the teaching of Arabic. Among its projects of note at present is a multidisciplinary university revolving around the Arab world and its language, culture and civilisation.

In truth, the role of the Institute could have been bigger had there been a better Arab response. From the outset, Arab countries have offered weak support, thus undermining the financial position of the Institute and the influence of Arab countries themselves on its policies.

The power of culture in our time has taken a new form based on persuasion and inducement. Culture, ideas, science and technology have the ability to facilitate communication and engagement among people. This leaves a mark in the form of new perceptions of the other, and dialogue and debate reveal the shared dreams of citizens of the world and their universal ways of life.

## The pillars of cultural diplomacy

The basic model of cultural diplomacy consists of four pillars: engaging with others, i.e. foreign policy; indirect influence through exported culture; interacting with entities other than states and official institutions such as civil society groups; and seeking long-term rather than short-term results.

In the introduction to a series of lectures on cultural diplomacy in New York, French cultural attaché Antonin Baudry[25] said: 'The purposes of cultural diplomacy are not cultural; they are part of foreign policy, whose means are education, research and culture. But while sending an ambassador is to recognise a power and build a state-to-state relationship, engaging in cultural diplomacy is to recognise, behind that power, a system of thought and establish a society-to-society relationship. Its challenge is to create, between two powers, rapports other than pressure, domination and an alliance of interests.'

Baudry argues that cultural diplomacy functions through three mechanisms: persuasion, inducement and education.

Persuasion and inducement, which are forms of soft power, are targeted at civil society and not just at institutions. Persuasion and inducement use all artistic and aesthetic means, including literature, art and film, to deliver cultural messages.

In effect, political institutions might oppose the work of cultural diplomacy, as happened during the Cold War with a Soviet ambassador in an African nation who did not get approval from the authorities in his country to distribute celebrated Soviet films such as Eisenstein's *Battleship Potemkin*, the Vasilyev brothers' *Chapaev* and Pudovkin's film based on Maxim Gorky's famous novel *Mother*. To allow people to see these films, the ambassador deliberately left the door of the film storage room at his residence open so that they might be stolen and shown to the public – this is according to French activist and director René Vautier. Vautier directed in 1950 *Afrique 50*, the first French anti-colonialism film, which was banned for over forty years, and for which Vautier was jailed for months.

History shows that persuasion and inducement may have a deeper impact than power and coercion, a case in point being what happened between the ancient Greek and Roman civilisations. As the Roman poet Horace put it: *Græcia capta ferum victorem cepit et artes Intulit agresti Latio.* The conquered Greece conquered her fierce conqueror and brought the arts into the rustic Latium.

The quote became famous for capturing the Greek cultural victory that eclipsed Rome's military triumph. Roman soldiers brought war and violence to Greece, while Greece brought theatre, poetry, architecture and philosophy to the Roman metropolis, which was simple and rustic at the time. While military victories determine political geography, cultural victories in the end shape intellects and influence behaviours and beliefs.

If we recall the magnificent ceremony that concluded the Olympic Games in Beijing in 2008, we will surely realise that soft power is intricately bound to the image a given culture projects. China presented an image of Chinese greatness, combining a glorious past when the country was one of the greatest civilisations in history, and a present when Chinese technology, investments and goods are sweeping the globe.

The ceremony, which left me astounded, was no random event. I am not talking here about the components of China's economic power, which are only one aspect of this country's strength. China has done its best to restore its archaeological monuments and preserve its tremendous heritage, and sought to include it in the UNESCO World Heritage lists. Equally interesting is that China has sought to develop its film industry, in line with South Korea and Japan's, to promote a joyful and pleasant image of China. In literature, a number of Chinese writers and novelists were immortalised by winning the Nobel Prize.

China has also paid attention to cultural institutions, led by the Confucius Institute, to spread Chinese culture, language, arts and music. China also allocates large resources to international aid and development. In short, China's cultural policy abroad is a great example that highlights the link between economic and cultural power, and the correlation between politics and culture in the context of soft power.

I look forward to seeing what my country will achieve during its hosting of the 2022 FIFA World Cup. It is not only a sports occasion but also a cultural festival that falls within the realm of cultural diplomacy, and will play an invaluable role in cementing the image of the country, society and culture in the minds of visitors. No doubt, Qatar is well aware of the importance of this challenge and its constructive role.

## Some instruments of cultural diplomacy

Cultural diplomacy is in essence about establishing relations between countries by means of culture, arts, science and education, with the goal of reaching mutual understanding, to use the language of diplomacy. Political scientist Milton Cummings defines cultural diplomacy as 'the exchange of ideas, information, art and other aspects of culture among nations and their peoples in order to foster mutual understandings'.[26]

However, this general perception requires an effort to develop it into a universal model for life and for values. Indeed, it is every nation's right to promote its history, symbols and culture.

Naturally, cultural diplomacy is based on cooperation between sovereign countries and recognised political entities, including ministries that represent governments and different cultural policies. Through formal relations between states, cultural diplomacy allows one culture to be introduced to another and for that country's perceptions, symbols and artistic creations to interact with those of the other.

At the same time, cultural diplomacy between nations seeks to build a shared symbolic space to enrich the self and the other, and pave the way for a dialectic of creativity among different cultures.

Some countries known for their distinguished cultural diplomacy have established institutions with an international character that vary in strength and influence. For instance, the Organisation internationale de la Francophonie (OIF) has access to considerable resources which it uses to promote the cultures of member states.

Governmental or independent civilian organisations also exist with substantial resources and targeted programmes for cultural diplomacy, aiming to forge links with intellectuals in other countries and encourage student exchange programmes and cultural and academic missions. In effect, personal relations play a key role in building international cultural networks and influencing public opinion.

France was a pioneer in establishing cultural organisations to promote her image abroad. In 1883, it founded the Alliance Française. Italy followed suit six years later with the Instituto Dante Alighieri, and then Britain, with the British Council in 1934. These organisations, which had an independent non–governmental character, have similar goals, namely to promote the national language and culture around the world and introduce a nation's way of life, arts, culture and science. Naturally, another ultimate goal behind these is projecting a positive image of the respective countries.

While we will not review the history of these hugely influential institutions in terms of cultural diplomacy, we should not forget the work of other organisations in the world that falls within this same broad category. Among them, for example, is the German Academic Exchange Service (DAAD) and the Goethe Institute, which also seek to promote the German language and facilitate academic cooperation. Another programme of note is the Fulbright Program, which has been active since the mid–twentieth century. The Fulbright seeks to promote culture, literature, arts and sciences through academic exchange. Nor should we overlook in the same vein South Korea's efforts to promote its language, drama, cinema and music, as popular inducements into Korean culture for young people around the world.

These various institutions are definitely part of the exercise of soft power, without being necessarily linked to government policy. Indeed, the efforts of states and their public diplomacy converge with those of these non-governmental organisations, whether they are backed by states such as the British Council or they are private initiatives such as the Fulbright Program. Whether their function is to expand the base of people who can speak a given language such as German, promote a culture like that of the French, or support education like the British Council, these initiatives are all examples of the convergence of culture, politics and diplomacy.

Recalling what we said at the beginning, that cultural diplomacy in essence is the establishment of relations between states by means of culture, art, science and education, we ought to consider one of the most prominent instruments of cultural diplomacy throughout human history, one that has carried the culture, art and knowledge of one people to another both overtly and covertly: the gift.

## The Diplomacy of Gifts

> 'Give gifts to love one another',
> -saying by the Prophet Muhammad.

A Chinese king is said to have once written to the Ummayad Caliph Muawiyah the following letter:

'The King of China wrote to Muawiyah:

From the King of Kings served by the daughters of a thousand kings, whose house was built with the milk of gold, who has a thousand elephants tethered, and who has two rivers watering aloe trees and eucalyptus whose scent travels for twenty miles.

To the King of the Arabs who worships God and associates no other with Him.

Greetings. I have sent you a gift, not a gift in any sense, but a masterpiece, so send me news of the permissible and the unlawful your prophet brought forth, and send someone to explain it to me. Peace.'[27]

The gift was a book containing the secrets of their knowledge. It is said that the book was bequeathed to Khalid bin Yazid bin Muawiyah thereafter, and from it he created great crafts.

The exchanges between rulers from different cultures in the Middle Ages had a special character. Gifts were a way of introducing cultures and knowledge, and their form and substance carried many connotations. In the example above, the friendly gift sent by the Chinese king inadvertently or otherwise introduced his people's tradition of book binding and writing, along with the craftsmanship and industry that went into the book and its contents. In return, the Chinese king asks Muawiyah to introduce him to the monotheistic religion that is different from his own, and, in addition, the tutor he asked to be sent would have taught him Arabic and Arabic writing and calligraphy.

## Fully featured acculturation

Cultural diplomacy in the Middle Ages took both amusing and refined forms as part of what art historians term the 'gift economy'. The exchanges under this economy developed in all directions, taking place between multiple parties, until they produced what art historian Oleg Grabar calls the 'culture of shared objects' between radically different cultures.

In this context, the objects are artefacts of various types and mediums, from ordinary pottery to precious stones to rare materials such as ivory from elephants or rhinos. These artefacts, some functional and others purely decorative, moved from one people to another through trade, but also as gifts exchanged between rulers.

The function of gifts in the political sphere was diplomatic, and yet it carried with it profoundly cultural messages. We can therefore say that artefacts exchanged as gifts were the fundamental expression of cultural diplomacy in the Middle Ages.

Arguably, the gift economy and the goods economy are both symbolic economies that complement one another, and sometimes even overlap or merge. But perhaps the fundamental difference between a gift and a commodity lies in the origin of each; while a merchant may buy goods from one country and sell them in another, the gift has to come from the country or culture that gives it. Ralph Waldo Emerson put it in more poetic terms:

> *Rings and other jewels are not gifts, but apologies for gifts. The only gift is a portion of thyself. Thou must bleed for me. Therefore the poet brings his poem; the shepherd, his lamb; the farmer, corn; the miner, a gem; the sailor, coral and shells; the painter, his picture; the girl, a handkerchief of her own sewing. This is right and pleasing, for it restores society in so far to the primary basis, when a man's biography is conveyed in his gift, and every man's wealth is an index of his merit.*[28]

There is an Arab anecdote about the civility required from the person presenting the gift, meaning that he must be well aware of the character and mentality of the recipient so that he does not accidentally insult or offend him, as is clear from Al-Mamoun's effort to examine a gift from Abu Duluf lest it contain something offensive to the women in his household.

> *Abu Duluf al-Qasim bin Isa al-Ijli sent Al-Mamoun, on Mihrajan Day, a gift of a hundred camel loads of saffron wrapped in floss silk nets on tamed grey she-onagers. The gift arrived while Al-Mamoun was with the female members (of the family). He was told that Al-Qasim bin Isa had dispatched a hundred loads of saffron on a hundred asses. Al-Mamoun wanted to see them as they were (still loaded), but he hated (the idea) that the asses would have something inappropriate for the women to see. Thus he asked this question about the asses: 'Are they she-asses or males?' The answer was that they were all tamed she-onagers, without a single male among them. He was happy (to hear) this, and said, 'I knew that*

*the man (Abu Duluf) was too clever to send (the gift) with anything but
she-asses!'*[29]

## The functions of the gift: traps, tests, knowledge exchange and historical witnesses

History has many stories about gifts that gained notoriety for different reasons. Perhaps some of the most famous gifts are the Trojan Horse, the gifts from the Queen of Sheba to Solomon and the gift from Caliph Harun al-Rashid to the King of France, the Holy Roman Emperor Charlemagne, in the Middle Ages.

The Trojan Horse is what we would call today a 'booby-trapped' or 'poisoned' gift. In essence, the gift is a token of love and friendship, but in the case of the Trojan Horse it was a deadly trap.

The legend of the Trojan Horse was first mentioned in Homer's *The Iliad*, one of the greatest epics of Western civilisation. Troy was a rival city that the Greeks tried to conquer for over a decade without success, thanks to its impregnable fortifications and resolute defence. The hero Ulysses decided to resort to deception instead of brute force, which had so far failed. The Greeks pretended to have failed in their expedition to take Troy and declared this publicly. Then they made a colossal wooden horse as a gift to the stubborn city, ostensibly to usher in a new era of peace and friendship.

Troy was pleased by the news, and opened its gates to pull the horse inside. There were celebrations and scenes of jubilation within the city of Troy, its citizens being unaware that some of the fiercest Greek warriors were concealed inside the horse. During the night, the Greeks stole out of the horse and massacred the unsuspecting Trojans, conquering the city and freeing their prisoners.

The Queen of Sheba's gift to Solomon, meanwhile, was a test to determine whether he was a king or a prophet, or whether his aims were worldly or religious. The Bible states: '1. When the Queen of Sheba heard about the fame of Solomon and his relationship to the Lord, she came to test Solomon with hard questions. 2. Arriving at Jerusalem with a very great caravan — with camels carrying spices, large quantities of gold, and precious stones — she came to Solomon and talked with him about all that she had on her mind.'

In the account given by the Quran of the encounter between the Queen of Sheba and Solomon, she tells her advisers:, 'In fact when the kings enter a town, they put it to disorder, and put its honorable citizens to disgrace, and this is how they normally do. And I am going to send a gift to them, then see, what response the envoys will bring back.'[30]

The biblical account presents a list of the gifts the Queen of Sheba gives to Solomon, including gold, large quantities of spices and precious stones. The Quranic account is different, and does not detail the nature of the gifts. But interpreters, including Al-Tabari, cite accounts specifying the gifts as slave girls and slave boys. Solomon is said to have ordered them to perform the ablutions to preserve their chastity.

Both accounts agree that the purpose of the gift was to test Solomon and verify whether he was a king or a prophet seeking to spread the faith. The Queen of Sheba would then decide: if the man were a prophet she would have no power to tempt him, but if he were a king he would be tempted by the gifts and would be no greater than her, and would not force her to give in to him.

Avinoam Shalem from the University of Munich[31] suggests that the movement of artefacts was a method by which historical information, real or contrived, was transmitted. He referred to those gifts and artefacts as 'relics of the past', meaning specific objects which clearly function as aides-memoires and help to keep specific events of our collective cultural memory fresh, in a manner in which a particular historical myth or account is constantly perpetuated. He further stated, 'The migration of such "relics of the past" from one cultural sphere to another is therefore extremely interesting for these items are the carriers of cultural knowledge.'

## Harun al-Rashid and Charlemagne

The story of Caliph Harun al-Rashid's gift to the Emperor Charlemagne is both culturally enlightening and amusing. Caliph Harun al-Rashid was a celebrated figure in Europe thanks to his diplomatic relations with the Holy Roman Emperor Charlemagne. They had exchanged ambassadors and engaged in various dealings, mentioned in the Royal Frankish Annals in the Carolingian period in AD 797–806. The gifts of Harun al-Rashid (whom the Franks called the king of Persia) were described as follows:

> They came to the emperor and delivered presents which the king of Persia sent to him, that is, a tent and curtains for the canopy of different colours and of unbelievable size and beauty. They were all made of the best linen, the curtains as well as the strings, and dyed in different colours. The presents of the Persian king consisted besides of many precious silken robes, of perfumes, ointments, and balsam; also of a brass clock, a marvellous mechanical contraption, in which the course of the twelve hours moved according to a water clock, with as many brazen little balls, which fall down on the hour and through their fall made a cymbal ring underneath. On this clock were also twelve horsemen who at the end of each hour stepped out of twelve windows, closing the previously open windows by their movements. There were many other things on this clock which are too numerous to describe now. Besides these presents there were two brass candlesticks of amazing size and height. All this was taken to the emperor in the palace at Aachen.

In his book about Harun al-Rashid,[32] Mansour Abdul-Hakim includes the following anecdote:

> The clock left the king and his entourage dumbfounded. The monks thought a demon resided in the clock, and at night, they brought axes and broke it

*apart, but found nothing inside except its mechanisms. King Charlemagne
was greatly saddened, and summoned scientists and skilled craftsmen to
repair it but they failed. Some of his advisers proposed that he ask Caliph
Harun al-Rashid to send an Arab delegation to fix it, but Charlemagne
said: 'I would feel deeply ashamed if the king in Baghdad learned that we
committed such a disgrace in the name of France.'*

The gift is a key element in diplomatic work, so much so that
countries give gifts budget allocations and dedicate special
departments for follow-up and monitoring. In democracies, official
gifts belong to the state.

Economically, gifts are hugely important in market economies,
especially around special occasions such as marriages and birthdays,
and holidays that vary between cultures and peoples.

## Culture and the rainbow of diplomacy

Fortunately for me, I was in charge of major diplomatic
missions in important cities such as Paris and New York before
I was entrusted with the cultural affairs of the State of Qatar.
Nevertheless, as I learned the ropes and worked hard to fulfil
the tasks entrusted to me, there was a general question that
preoccupied me more and more as I moved in the diplomatic
community: what common ground could we build upon? How
could we reduce the distance between us and the differences in
our goals and interests and expand the space for agreement? This
was the challenge between local and global concerns, between
self-interest and humanitarianism: How could we be here and
there at the same time?

Perhaps like many diplomats, I have always been fundamentally
an optimist who sees the glass as half full. This is not on account
of wishful thinking but by necessity, because diplomacy is
nothing if it is not the art of convergence, understanding and
collaboration.

Perhaps one of the most interesting opportunities that is made available to a diplomat is the chance to embrace multilateral diplomacy. I was lucky to serve as my country's permanent envoy at the United Nations and before it at UNESCO, where I saw and appreciated the true meaning of collective diplomatic action. In these forums, the multiplicity of parties involved and of terms of reference force each party to conduct itself in a positive spirit regardless of intent and differences in interests. The nature of the work makes each party need the other, as the voting is ultimately a secret vote. There is no room in this context to impose views, no matter how strong any party is and irrespective of its calculations. This means relying on persuasion and argument to convince all others – or at least a majority of those who will vote.

In fact, one of the characteristics of multilateral diplomacy is its reliance on acquaintance and engagement. Every representative of a state knows other representatives personally, making collective action a strange combination of the interests of countries and regional blocs, personal relations, shared tastes and attitudes, rational thinking and mutual interests.

We now live in a time where culture cannot thrive except within a coherent and integrated system of human development. Any imbalance in this system, when the requirements of cultural creativity are no longer satisfied, leads inevitably to placing culture at the bottom of the list of priorities.

## The direction of the compass

In the aftermath of the Second World War, humanity gave out clear indications that it was starting to understand the harsh lessons of the war, notably with the creation of the United Nations. The establishment of the international organisation was an explicit declaration that that collective rationality required managing discussions and differences, as difficult and complicated as the task was, instead of indulging in barbarism that no longer befitted the human race and its level of intelligence. The direction of the compass needed to be changed.

UNESCO, with its emphasis on culture, science and education, is probably the most prominent component of the new agenda to change the world. The aim is to forge a new history based on a set of principles, ethics and norms that reflect the dreams of the peoples of the world.

UNESCO represents a bid to go beyond local and national cultures to the broader horizons of global culture. This would not have happened were it not for the gradual shift towards a collective mentality focusing on shared and universal human values. In that respect, UNESCO is a forum for dialogue about humanity's future, based on multilateral diplomacy, science, education and culture.

In truth, changing the direction of the compass was not just a declaration of intent, though bringing about change requires many resources led by funding. Let us recall here, as an example, the huge education initiative undertaken by UNESCO in the 1960s.

UNESCO understood that changing minds is the path to changing the status quo, and invested in human development, linking investment in education to economic development. At the time, this was not obvious or the subject of consensus. Nevertheless, UNESCO fought that battle in harmony with the United Nations Development Program. Thanks to this vision, millions of children were able to go to school and open up new horizons intellectually and socially.

Despite some setbacks caused by funding problems and conflicting views on development, the dynamism that began in the 1960s has demonstrated what cultural diplomacy can achieve through theory and practice by establishing an international organisation for culture and education based on successful and effective models, and profound visions linking global principles to local traditions.

With such projects, humanity entered a new and promising era for the future of humankind. Behind all this, however, are the new trends in multilateral cultural diplomacy.

## On the new global cultural diplomacy

It should be pointed out that the presence of non-governmental organisations and civil society in cultural diplomacy is nothing new, even in bilateral diplomacy. This is part of a local and global trend linked to efforts to strike a balance between 'political society' and 'civil society' in every country with a democratic system, whose polity integrates various constituencies.

Scholars have observed that the political shift in cultural diplomacy occurred in the wake of the First World War. But most of the manifestations of this diplomacy were undertaken by individuals or groups of artists, explorers, travellers, intermediaries or even invaders. Most of them were not official state institutions. As a result, the free exchange of information and images between cultures resulting from those efforts could be said to be a pre-cultural diplomacy phase.[33] The absence of official channels and a planned cultural strategy, along with the ambiguity of the goals, make these rather individual efforts.

When the interests of countries and their diplomacy required establishing cultural diplomacy in its modern institutional form, the relationship between government action and independent cultural civil organisations grew and expanded. For example, the British Council, despite being an independent organisation, works in collaboration with the British government, which specifies which countries it should operate in. Likewise, the federal government in Germany guides cultural efforts by drafting policies and allocating resources in collaboration with independent entities such as the Goethe Institute. This way, the work of non-governmental and independent organisations complements the work of their governments.[34]

This trend linked to state policies led to arguments that cultural diplomacy should be independent from governments. In essence, cultural diplomacy is cultural exchange with foreign entities on behalf of the nation and the people. People felt they should themselves address their peers in the target countries, and set themselves the goals and activities, a position that was a reaction to the monopoly by the states on the mechanisms and aims of cultural exchange. This stance made some governments paranoid about non-governmental organisations and civil society in general, as their interests might not be aligned to those of the government, not to mention the difficulty of monitoring and steering them.

In fact, and unlike with other areas, no country can engage in cultural diplomacy without strong support from non-governmental cultural players, be they teachers, lecturers, students, artists or authors,[35] even if they have different goals from those of official government agencies.

In all cases, civil society and non-governmental organisations have demonstrated their competence in forging solid and lasting relations based on dialogue, understanding and mutual trust with individuals and organisations in other countries. In addition, these non-governmental organisations are better able to secure the trust of the target audience, because the conventional approach by governments to cultural diplomacy has raised questions regarding legitimacy and neutrality. People are wary, and are not interested in anything other than a cultural engagement based on mutual respect.

Thus, the experience of UNESCO in multilateral cultural diplomacy offers an important lesson for bilateral cultural diplomacy. There is no alternative to interaction between governments and civil society, including non-governmental and independent organisations, or to forging real partnerships between them and funded companies and individual partnerships to achieve the goals set out in cultural exchange programmes and initiatives directed at any foreign audience.[36]

We do not see any contradiction between bilateral and multilateral cultural diplomacy. Both play an invaluable role in bringing people together and supporting cultural dialogue, if built on respecting cultural diversity, dialogue and commitment to freedom, human rights, ethics and social responsibility through culture.

# Chapter Six
# Consultations as a Cultural Phenomenon

## Political disputes and cultural differences

In 1984, I moved from one of the most culturally and artistically significant capitals of the world, Paris, to a city with a different kind of political and cultural allure, New York City. But New York was not a city that opened its doors easily into its treasures of knowledge, which meant that I had to invest much time and effort to persuade the Big Apple to let me into its heart.

In Paris, I had tried to continue my higher education and registered myself in a PhD programme, but in the end did not have time to complete it.

I continued to have an irresistible desire to obtain my doctorate. As soon as I settled in New York, I started English language courses so as to be able to progress at university. A long but enjoyable journey began of contacting universities until I was able to enrol in the State University of New York at Stony Brook, on the outskirts of New York City.

In parallel with this commitment, I had enormous responsibilities in my capacity as Qatar's permanent representative to the United Nations in what was a very delicate time. War was raging in our region between the neighbouring nations of Iraq and Iran. I had to find a solution to my personal dilemma of continuing my doctorate research and following this great tragedy in our region that carried huge risks for all its countries.

The foreign ministers of the Arab Gulf states were aware of the critical nature of the situation. They were permanent guests at the UN Security Council, trying to resolve that thorny issue, which required me always to be present with my foreign minister for counsel and assistance as well.

I finished the core theoretical courses at the university. After consulting with my doctorate supervisor, we agreed on a topic that would combine my daily functions and relevant studies. After some thinking, the topic I chose was 'Decision-Making at the UN Security Council: The Iraq–Iran War as a Case Study'. The study lasted longer than expected because of my preoccupations. My work at the United Nations was extended for another year, and in the end I did not present my doctoral dissertation until 1990, when I was ambassador in Washington, DC.

In truth, I found it difficult to gather references for the core topic of my dissertation, as they were notably scarce. I would even argue that the dissertation itself became a useful reference in Arabic on decision-making processes at the Security Council.

## Consultations

In international diplomacy, personal feelings and concerns sometimes influence diplomatic work. This is what happened when Javier Pérez de Cuéllar, the UN Secretary General at the time, visited Qatar in 1985, war still raging between Iraq and Iran.

On Pérez de Cuéllar's first meeting with His Highness Sheikh Khalifa bin Hamad Al Thani, Emir of the State of Qatar at the time, I wrote in my doctoral thesis:

> It is well established that the important meeting between the Secretary General of the United Nations and His Highness Sheikh Khalifa Al Thani, [former] Emir of the State of Qatar, had a decisive impact on arranging a visit by the

*Secretary General to both Tehran and Baghdad. The author of this study – as the head of Qatar's delegation to the United Nations – attended this meeting in Doha, following a visit by the secretary general to Riyadh and other Gulf nations. When the Emir of Qatar asked the secretary general whether he was planning to visit Baghdad and Tehran, he said that he did not intend to do so during his current visit. At this point, the Emir of Qatar explained that without visiting these two countries, the main parties to the war, the tour would not achieve its goals. The secretary general replied that he could not undertake the visit without guarantees regarding the possibility of a ceasefire, to avoid causing further frustration in the world public opinion. The Emir of Qatar said that even if the visit did not achieve direct and tangible results, it would definitely be an important step along the way towards implementing a ceasefire. As the meeting drew to an end, the secretary general appeared like he had gradually started to accept the former emir's proposals, but pointed out that there were two obstacles: one, that he could not go to Iraq and Iran unless they agree to a ceasefire during his visit; and two, that he needed a safe transport to the two countries. The emir here offered the secretary general his private plane, and the UN chief agreed to the offer. This was followed by successful contacts via New York to secure the approval of Iraq and Iran to a ceasefire during the visit. Later on, the visit [to Qatar] proved to have been extremely important for achieving the long-sought goal of a ceasefire.[37]*

You can imagine my feelings of responsibility for the safety of the secretary general as he visited the two capitals when war was raging fiercely between them, since it was we in Qatar who had convinced him to make that visit. Bear in mind that planes are often hit during conflicts, intentionally or unintentionally. I did not feel relieved and reassured until the man had returned safely, and I received him at the airport in Doha as though he had been born again – and I born again with him.

## Informal consultations

Resolving an issue lies in reaching a decision following official consultations between relevant parties. But in most cases, the parties do not reach the desired solution or decision through these official discussions, which are often accompanied by tension, short deadlines and stubborn positions that hinder compromise. I believe many experts and scholars would agree with me when I say that solutions mostly come through secret consultations, contacts and mediations, in which negotiators have greater freedom and access to decision makers, without being concerned about public opinion and one-upmanship from rivals and other parties participating in the negotiations.

I saw it fit to dedicate a chapter in my PhD thesis to diplomatic consultations and their implications. This was not easy, as I could not find reliable references in this regard. I thus resorted to direct observations of consultations as a participant and a witness at the Security Council and the United Nations in general, and in various consultations I took part in throughout my diplomatic career. For this reason, I chose to overview in this book some of my conclusions on the issue of consultations, a political phenomenon related to dialogue between parties who often come from different cultures. Furthermore, consultations have a role in finding solutions not only to political disputes but also to cultural, economic, social and other issues.

## Patterns of consultation

Informal consultations at the Security Council are characterised by flexibility and secrecy. Meetings are held without an official agenda and off the record, and, of course, without media coverage. Nevertheless, there are specific procedures, and usually the president of the Security Council calls these meetings, which are held in several different venues, and makes the necessary arrangements.

Concerning attendance, reports indicate that informal consultations do not kick off until the fifteen members of the Security Council are present, in addition to the secretary general and his aides. It has never happened that any were excluded. Reports also show that many times Security Council members launch bilateral consultations, since talks between a smaller number of parties may be more spontaneous and candid.

At the same time, non-members in the Security Council may attend these consultations, including representatives of regional movements and national liberation organisations.

Concerning the timing, informal consultations are often held prior to, on the sidelines of, after, or even during official Security Council meetings to consider a specific issue. It may be technically difficult to hold both formal and informal meetings at the same time, though some experts believe simultaneous representation in both formal and informal sessions may allow for a broader consensus.

It is worth mentioning that there are no official records for informal consultations, although it is common for Security Council members to take notes. Although there is no standard way to brief the media on these discussions, some information reaches media outlets on occasion, and the president of the Security Council, based on his or her judgement, may agree to answer questions from the press. While the president of the Security Council in general can provide information on the activities of the Council, he or she cannot discuss the topics being debated in informal discussions. In any case, it may be prudent for the president to issue an official statement in some form on known consultations, instead of leaving the matter to the rival parties or to speculation by media outlets.

## The traditions of consultations

The traditions at the UN Security Council, especially those set out by Woodrow Wilson, call for holding public agreements reached by the members openly. But informal consultations contradict this principle. Although necessity knows no law and renders consultations as such crucial, caveats apply, including the risk that the Security Council could become an exclusive club for the major powers, which would reach deals among themselves through secret consultations behind closed doors. This brings to mind the fact that Dag Hammarskjöld,[38] the assassinated secretary general who considered himself an advocate for the rights of small states, feared that the secret work of the Security Council could reinforce its image as an exclusive club for the major powers.

Brian Urquhart, a long-serving senior United Nations official, mentioned an additional reason to be concerned about informal consultations, which he said could prolong negotiations unnecessarily. He warned that informal procedures allow intransigent parties to cling to their positions, and may render the Security Council more reluctant to hold a formal meeting. This way, the Council is practically turned into a place for 'whispering behind closed doors on issues that concern international peace and security'.

A report by the secretary general on the work of the United Nations in 1982, drafted by Kurt Waldheim and presented by the new secretary general, Javier Pérez de Cuéllar, alluded to the increased use of unofficial consultations, but warned afterwards that this process could become an alternative to action by the Security Council or even an excuse for inaction.

## Consultations in the balance

Despite the potential concerns and caveats, diplomats and UN officials in general believe that the higher frequency of informal consultations is a positive development in the work of the Security Council. Concerning claims by some that these consultations are responsible for the paralysis of the Security Council, some respond by asking how national delegations could reach consensus in public but not in private; they argue that whispering behind closed doors is better than yelling through open doors. History has shown that UN Security Council decisions do not necessarily lead to measures, meaning that some resolutions are mere formalities meant to appease all sides even if not all are convinced by them, because consultations were public and informal consultations absent.

Yet informal consultations are a complex subject and could be abused by many parties. Despite the lack of verified studies from within the organisation about this procedural development, informal consultations are worthy of study as part of a deeper and longer-lasting examination of procedures.

Nevertheless, G.R. Berridge Berridge's[39] opinion involves a dose of certainty. 'If the Security Council fails to reach an agreement in a private meeting, then there would be no diplomatic worth in declaring its differences in public. This would have no other result than to push every side to cling on to its stance, poison the climate, and expose the council for being unable to act.' Most diplomats believe that 'the prevailing view is that the failure to act is better than to act without doing proper research.'[40]

In sum, informal consultations at the Security Council play both positive and negative roles. Consensus among permanent members is more likely even if the issue is sensitive and complex, and affects the interests of one or more Council members. But from the point of view of non-permanent members of the Council, the greater leeway in times of crisis through informal talks may come at the expense of their smaller contributions.

## The decision-making process

Individual decision makers face many obstacles preventing the achievement of ideal or even logical results. The obstacles become more complex when the decision maker in question is a multilateral organisation such as the Security Council, which in turn consists of entities representing multilateral decision makers.

In addition, the power of veto enjoyed by the five permanent members of the Security Council adds another layer of complexity to the decision-making process. Thus, the requirements of an agreement or non-objection among the five permanent members have often been an obstacle to the Council fulfilling its responsibilities under the Charter of the United Nations.

If we want to express this in a diplomatic way, we could say that the veto right was never consistent with the responsibility of the Security Council in maintaining international peace and security. No doubt the veto power was in many cases, as far as international security is concerned, the fuse in the fuse box, preventing the escalation of serious confrontations among major powers to the point of ignition. But reality and historical truth also suggest the veto power was often wielded in accordance with narrow national interests.

The tension that has marred international relations has revived hopes of re-emphasising the intentions of the founders of the United Nations, who wanted the collective power of the international community to protect weak parties from the aggressive plans of strong parties. The fear remains, however, that the strong parties will be in a position to use reforms to impose their own vision for the new world order on the weaker parties.

It is worthwhile recalling now, in the second decade of the twenty-first century, the main objective of the United Nations as set forth in Article I, paragraph 1, of the Charter: 'To maintain international peace and security, and to that end: to take effective collective measures for the prevention and removal of threats to the peace, and for the suppression of acts of aggression or other breaches of the peace, and to bring about by peaceful means, and in conformity with the principles of justice and international law, adjustment or settlement of international disputes or situations which might lead to a breach of the peace.'

In light of the difficulties that have historically hindered the United Nations and the Security Council in fulfilling this purpose, the international community has resorted to culture and cultural diplomacy to diagnose the problem. This is not new in reality, as UNESCO in 1949 issued a report prepared by a panel of experts on the comparative studies of cultures, which said: 'The problem of international understanding is a problem of the relationship between cultures. From this relationship a new society should emerge based on mutual understanding and respect. This society must take on a new humanitarian form, so that its universality may be achieved through the recognition of common values across different cultures.'

I believe that more than six decades later, this excellent notion continues to be a roadmap for humankind, and we must acknowledge that humanity has achieved some of these goals since then.

## Lost in cultural translation

Consultations are no doubt closely linked to culture. Interlocutors are often from different cultures, each culture playing a role in the respective interlocutor's style and discourse. Therefore, rapprochement between cultures is an essential element for convergence during negotiations of any kind. Translation and interpreting reflects a real-life example of diverse cultural backgrounds interacting to reach agreements through meetings, consultation and negotiation. Here, the accuracy and quality of translation are extremely important, in light of misunderstandings that may otherwise occur, poison the negotiating climate or hinder agreement.

A funny anecdote in this regard involves former Qatari Foreign Minister Sheikh Ahmed bin Saif Al Thani, when he was in a meeting with his Soviet counterpart to discuss the Iraq–Iran war and a resolution of the conflict. The interpreter was Russian. We were surprised when the Russian interpreter suddenly announced that the Iraqis and Iranians must swap *al-asirra* – Arabic for 'beds'. The minister turned to me and said with a smile: 'What do beds have anything to do with this?' Of course, the interpreter meant to say *al-asra*, or prisoners.

I once expressed admiration for the Arabic linguistic abilities of a skilled Russian interpreter. He told me with a smile: 'I only know little compared to your great linguist Sibawayh, who carried with him ten camel loads of books. If I gathered all my books together, I would need no more than one camel to carry them.'

We cannot mention anecdotes about translation without recalling what happened to the interpreter Igor Korchilov, who interpreted at meetings between George H. W. Bush and Mikhail Gorbachev, as he noted it in his book *Translating History*. The two sides were locked in intensive talks to reach an agreement on arms control and the two leaders were discussing details on how each party would verify the other's arsenal. There was a divergence over which party's aircraft would be used to verify the agreement. The Americans wanted the planes to come from the party that requested verification (the verifying party) while the Russians wanted the planes to come from the party being verified. The interpreter misheard Gorbachev and interpreted his condition as 'the verifying party'. Everyone was surprised by the sudden shift in the Russian position and turned to the interpreter, who quickly corrected his mistake. He writes: 'Everyone now turned their heads to look at me. At that moment, I wished the earth could swallow me up. Someone once said that "good interpretation is like air – no one notices it until it is polluted". Nobody notices the interpreter as long as he is doing all right, but the moment he makes a slip, he becomes the focus of attention.'

Korchilov concludes with another anecdote: 'After the session was over, I went up to Bush to apologise for the blunder. He heard me out, patted me on the shoulder, and quipped, 'But you didn't start World War Three!' Gobachev, too, took it in his stride. "The costs of interpretation," he said graciously, and concluded, "He who does nothing makes no mistakes."'[41]

# Chapter Seven
# Dialogue between Cultures

When you enter any airport in the world, or walk around any major city, at first glance, despite the convergence of so many people who seem to have little in common, beneath it all they are very similar. These people, even if a notion of brotherhood among people may seem overly idealistic, will at the very least board the same plane or train, or spend the afternoon in the same park.

Boarding a plane has become an ordinary and routine practice that no longer causes wonder about this strange invention and the complicated path that freed humanity from the chains of gravity.

The legend of Icarus and his father, the shrewd inventor Daedalus, as narrated by Ovid, alludes to man's dream to free himself from the chains tying him to the ground. It is a story about humanity's quest to soar in the sky against all danger and risk, driven by the desire to discover and travel to the heavens.

Icarus's wings were crafted from wax and feathers, and they melted as soon as he flew close to the sun. But humanity's dream to fly continued until the forebears of Daedalus, a figurehead of technology by which man sought to tame the world, were able to realise it.

Another symbolic implication of the aeroplane that concerns us is that it is a means by which people may rise up physically, morally and culturally. The path of humanity is strewn with illuminated signs, despite the pains, the setbacks and the wrong turns. In this context, cultural diplomacy is one instrument that accelerates our emancipation from existing constraints towards our desired destination.

No doubt all cultures have similar versions of this dream which, today, thanks to scientific and technological progress, is a reality. We enjoy its fruits to the point that we have forgotten that, only a few decades ago, flying was in the realm of fantasy.

We are also distracted by the details of modern life and our entrenched habits and forget that we, on planes, live different rituals and experience a world of its own with its special rules and etiquette.

The aeroplane is an international space that unites us and sets rule for convivial coexistence throughout the period of the journey. It is not a space where we are or should be burdened by our cultural idiosyncrasies and social habits, our inherited language, or our notions of familiar roads, yet at the same time it is not completely disconnected from all of that. It is a delicate balance between holding on to individual and cultural identity, and compelling the voluntary traveller to embark on an adventure – with his safety preserved – in crossing from one airport or city to another.

On the plane, we learn safety instructions in the event of a plane crash, God forbid, a ritual that for those of us who have travelled frequently is almost a habit and a formality. But let us each remember our first plane trip, and the circumstantial alienation we felt as we prepared for new rules, even if they were temporary. All this proves that people, with their symbolic baggage and individual and cultural habits, could overcome themselves and what they are familiar with to cross into another place, in the process acquiring a new culture shared with other unknown passengers.

People thus find themselves in a real communicative position that compels them to rid themselves of negative attitudes and adapt to a new microcosm. The process is similar to the need to accept the diversity of our own community and to understand the symbols of others without sacrificing our own self-consciousness.

A well-made anti-racism video went viral on social media not long ago. Produced by the Portuguese Commission to celebrate the fiftieth anniversary of the Universal Declaration of Human Rights, the video can be found online[42].

A middle-aged woman on a plane finds out that she is sitting next to a black man. She is appalled and asks the flight attendant to find her another seat. The flight attendant asks her to wait while she consults the captain.

The flight attendant returns seconds later and tells the woman, 'The captain said he was able to find a seat in first class. He also apologises because it's incredible a passenger has to travel beside such a despicable person.' Just as the woman starts to stand up, visibly pleased, the flight attendant turns to the man and says, 'Sir, will you please follow me?'

The clever video then concludes the surprising twist by appealing to the viewer to put racism in its rightful place.

## The butterfly effect

The microcosm of the plane can serve as a metaphor for the larger world. The history of humankind bears witness that we are in a continuous journey from one port to another, coexisting along the way with other faiths, races, colours and ideas.

In addition to diversity among groups, identities in the individualistic modern world can also be diverse. Diversity requires individuals and communities to develop abilities and skills that help them respect others on an ongoing basis, and add nuance to their inherited values, customs, symbols, traditions and perceptions of humanity, the Divine and the world. People and communities are compelled to strike a balance between their personalities and

133

harmony with others. There can be no peace in our culturally diverse and globalised world except through this and through cross-cultural communication skills.

I am not adding anything new when I say that the peoples of our world today are like crowds of aeroplane passengers boarding the same aircraft. The effect of a flutter of a butterfly in the East may conceivably help cause a major event in the West, and vice versa. This 'butterfly effect' in global culture has many consequences, especially with the unprecedented revolution in global communications. Indeed, which culture can claim today to be pure from any outside influences?

I am not talking here only about major cultures such as India and China, the Arab world and the West. I am also – or especially – talking about the cultures of smaller communities and even isolated ones living in remote places.

While cultural diversity is a fact that needs no effort to establish, highlighting, promoting and respecting it is not necessarily that obvious or self-evident. What is more difficult still is developing a deep feeling of belonging to shared human culture inclusive of pluralism and diversity. Herein lies the greatest challenge, as is clear in the UNESCO programme International Decade for a Culture of Peace and Non-violence for the Children of the World (IDCP).[43] The challenge is to protect the plane of humanity as it flies in a clouded, turbulent sky, and ensure its passengers a comfortable and enjoyable trip to safety.

Spreading a culture of peace and non-violence is a major aim we believe cultural diplomacy should help achieve. One – if not the most important – of pathways to do this is dialogue between cultures and the conditions, preparations and instruments it requires. Cultural diversity is the airport our metaphorical plane takes off from, and intercultural citizenship achieved through dialogue is its destination.

# On cultural diversity and globalisation

If we look at globalisation objectively, we find it to be the fruit of several economics-based mechanisms. Globalisation has linked the world together in the same way the Internet has done with global communication, virtually and in the real world.

The comparison is not random. The Internet itself, if we look at its history, appears to be part of globalisation or one of its manifestations. Yet the main point of comparison is that communications are controlled by known monopolies and carry several disadvantages as well as advantages. The same applies to globalisation. It is naïve to see it as an absolute positive because economic, technological and scientific facts prove it is a manifestation of 'unequal development', to quote Samir Amin. The so-called digital gap is clear proof of this.

When we focus on the cultural face of globalisation, while bearing in mind its links to the strategies of hegemony, we will understand that cultural diplomacy cannot remain oblivious to its implications and its effects. Never before have relations between cultures been as intricate as they are today, with the clear result of this putting borders between cultures and national economies into question, with serious implications indeed.

Let us first remember that the extensive communication between cultures, as much as it has opened up broad horizons has left those cultures that are not backed by scientific, technological and economic progress out in the open, making them more vulnerable. For this reason, globalisation has been somewhat of a threat to smaller cultures and cultural identities, especially those that have been unable to self-progress by linking their past and their heritage to an innovative present inspired by scientific and technological progress.

Some of these cultures resemble endangered animal species or artefacts preserved in museums. At best, they are like rare monuments and antiquities that have not received enough care and funding to preserve them.

Some peoples, when they feel threatened, will revert to their distinctive identities. In doing so, they may fiercely defend their symbols, making those identities 'deadly identities',[44] as Amin Maalouf said, engaging with global influences with a reactionary logic. This is what we have seen, in different forms and degrees, in the former Yugoslavia and even in ancient civilisations such as India.

This painful reality, however, will not stop the sweeping tide and all its positive aspects – meaning the current that is pushing for closer bonds and bridges between cultures. For this reason, it requires managing this diversity to steer it in the direction of building a shared future protecting each culture and including it in dynamic, sustainable development efforts. It is indispensable for any serious cultural diplomacy to engage in this collective humanitarian dream.

Humankind has enough common tools and values to prepare for this noble diplomatic mission. In its essence, it is an act of negotiation geared towards building mutually agreed stances, perceptions and understandings. It is also a quintessentially cultural act that requires good communication and debating skills.

In effect, dealing with the issue of diversity and globalisation from the standpoint of cultural diplomacy is based on a rich international legal system that facilitates it and makes agreement on many issues possible. I do not want to burden the reader with the literature in this regard, but will make brief references to the international legal system that frames cultural diplomacy, at least at the institutional level.

The Universal Declaration of Human Rights is a good starting point, by virtue of its international legal and moral strength and status, for institutional intercultural dialogue. It is no coincidence that education is the entryway to achieving a balance between the individual's cultural personality and promoting tolerance and understanding between cultures and peoples. Article 26, paragraph 2 of the Declaration states: 'Education shall be directed to the full development of the human personality and to the strengthening of respect for human rights and fundamental freedoms. It shall promote understanding, tolerance and friendship among all nations, racial or religious groups, and shall further the activities of the United Nations for the maintenance of peace.'

We notice that this paragraph sets out an ideal and identifies education as the means to achieve it. If we translate these grand principles into actions that we can negotiate internally and between countries, they will require enormous efforts and strategies as well as international solidarity, especially in the complicated field of education.

The Universal Declaration of Human Rights also contains a number of principles linked to civil, political, economic, social and cultural rights that support this international orientation.

The balance between cultural diversity and celebrating local traditional culture and the global nature of the principles of human rights charters guides all negotiations in the context of cultural diplomacy. Human rights and cultural diplomacy are continuously interacting, rendering intercultural dialogue a genuine path to collective human development.

Respecting human rights standards and creating a medium conducive to individual and public freedoms can also represent a solid framework for cultural dialogue to thrive in.

Any culture is the product of an internal dialogue and a negotiated path that has led it to coalesce around a given form. The Arab culture is a good example in this respect. This great culture was formed because of historic events and processes that produced what some have termed the 'Arab mind'.[45] Regardless of the implications and criticisms of this concept,[46] what matters is the general idea that this culture is the result of negotiations between many intellectual movements that all contributed to developing it.

The rich and diverse reality of Arab culture, which at its height gave the world a great deal of knowledge, technological innovations, philosophical ideas and literary masterpieces, is the result of interactions from Asia to Africa and the Mediterranean, as Arab culture negotiated with different cultures with which it made contact throughout history.

The Arabs came into close contact with the products of great cultures, including those of Persia, India and Greece. But the Arabs also engaged with others beyond these geographically close cultures, as we read in the chronicles of Arab explorers and travellers, who introduced their own cultures and learned about others'.

These writings represented one mechanism of the dialogue encouraged by the Prophet's respect for other faiths. Islam is the continuity of these faiths, all part of a system by which God addresses his creation. Respect for other faiths and the self-possession it requires are the mainstay of cultural humility. Islam is part of the monotheistic religions, and part of the religious phenomenon's historic progression and different points of view, which have allowed the existence of diverse spiritual and religious systems – the embodiment of the Quranic verse 'O mankind! We created you from a single pair of a male and a female, and made you into nations and tribes, that ye may know each other. Verily the most honoured of you in the sight of Allah is the most righteous of you. And Allah has full knowledge and is well acquainted with all things.'[47]

Cultural diplomacy needs such authentic models rooted in the history of the Arabs, and of other cultures and peoples, to guide us and serve as proof that we have a solid foundation upon which to build. This holds true even if the strategies to do so have changed, and the negotiating parameters and methods have improved thanks to the United Nations and its agencies. The idea of cultural diplomacy in terms of intercultural dialogue is now based on a solid institutional foundation led by UNESCO.

Institutionalisation is necessary for the success of international negotiations. This was what was perhaps absent from historical cultural diplomacy and dialogue, whose purpose is global citizenship. What is important to emphasise is that the shared human rights legacy, embodied by the international human rights system, is the moral and legal cradle of international cultural diplomacy. We cannot imagine a stronger reference frame or language for dialogue between nations and cultures than the language of human rights.

## Cultural identities and global citizenship

The challenge today is not just to preserve the spiritual and physical features of cultural groups, including their arts, literature, values, traditions and way of life. We also see in all cultures another trend that needs to be addressed: cultural identities in our world today are undergoing internal changes because of external influences that we may not be able to deal with before it is too late.

If we consider cultural transformations in relation to women's issues and the social roles of men and women, for example, we will see that all cultures are witnessing a shift in their system of values related to gender. The shift is the result of women entering spheres that were not traditionally open to them, generating new concepts and different views of women. When girls go to school, for example, cultural values immediately shift, and society's view of them gradually evolves, along with the values a given culture assigns to women and girls.

This observation is free of any value judgement. In other words, the old situation in traditional societies is not necessarily better, nor is the new situation in modern societies necessarily worse, as Amal al-Qarami indicates.[48] The point about the example of women and cultural values, including traditions, values and beliefs concerning women, is that cultural identity is variable and dynamic.

Equality between men and women has become a shared global cultural endeavour, for which policies and programmes are being developed to empower women in various aspects of life, from culture and politics to the economy. The shift is the result of interaction between cultures, proving that it is impossible to keep any culture isolated from the influence of other cultures.

The great dilemma here is this, however: how do local cultures and traditions become useful resources for building a shared human outlook?

Whether we like it or not, we are moving towards a type of citizenship that crosses cultures, or, rather, towards an intercultural citizenship. The convergence among nations and peoples, thanks to scientific exchange and international cooperation, has gradually started to impose something similar to what we described, when people meet at an airport to board the same plane.

Global values have led to this intercultural citizenship, where people, both in words and deeds, care for and defend the rights of other countries' citizens and cultures. One of these global values is thus global responsibility that transcends identities, cultures and geographical distance. How else can we explain protests by one country's citizens against war in another? Or when civil society groups rush to offer assistance during natural disasters to other communities? What about the international civilian groups working to mitigate poverty or disease, and defending the environment or the freedom of the press?

Isolationism and retreating into one's identity because of globalisation's hegemony is in the end a crude expression of a culture of fear, and of a stale perception of what constitutes culture.

Yet this kind of reaction is proof that all cultures are experiencing shifts and transformations. Cultures have inevitably become hybrid, whether consciously or otherwise. The current complexity in knowledge and cultural hybridisation is unprecedented in the history of humankind, and no one can predict what the final outcome will be.

For this reason, cultural diplomacy needs to proceed from a crucial contemplative distance, and answer questions about this shared destiny and steer it to prevent it from veering out of control.

What we are examining here is the spontaneous willingness to engage in intercultural citizenship among broad segments around the world. This is in our view positive and important, and cultural diplomacy must build on it to resist violence, hatred, racism, discrimination, anti-Semitism and Islamophobia and to promote a culture of peace among peoples.

We are truly on board the same plane, and need to make sure we will reach our destination in the best conditions. If this happens, each one of us will return to his or her identity and culture, having been enriched by new values, the adoption of which will help renew and develop all cultures in the direction of national and international coexistence.

We are witnessing the birth of a new human being who is both a citizen of his culture and a citizen of the world who interacts with other cultures. Cultural diplomacy has a noble mission here: help bring about this new universal human.

# Chapter Eight
# Education: The Road to Freedom

A wealthy pearl merchant had a son who was very bright. As the folk tale goes, he taught him from an early age how to trade pearls in his city, until he had imparted all his experience to the youth. When the boy had grown and fully matured, the father decided to send him travelling to expand business, giving him money, supplies and a bag of pearls. The son set off in search of a living.

The son set sail, then travelled on foot for a couple of days. He was soon exhausted, and at night-time one day decided to rest in a meadow. Before he fell asleep, he noticed an old fox lying on the ground, unable to move. The boy stared at him and asked himself: how will this poor beast be able to eat? He reckoned the fox would soon die of hunger.

The boy was immersed in his thoughts when a lion came along, dragging a heavy carcass that he started to eat near the fox. When he had finished, he left the remains and moved away. The old fox stood up and crawled over to the prey, and in turn ate until he was full. The boy watched in surprise, pondering the work of fate that brought food to the old fox, without his having to run and hunt for it. The boy sat up and told himself: if fate brought sustenance in this manner, why should I face hardship and risk travel to make a living? He spent the night in the meadow and then returned home in the morning. When he told his father how he came to be dissuaded from travelling, his elderly father said, 'Son, you were observant but you lacked insight. I wanted you to be the lion on whom hungry foxes count, not a hungry fox who waits for lions to eat their leftovers!'

This story from our heritage demonstrates that education is not just about imparting the skills of reading and writing. It is essentially educating people to have morals, ethics, values and ideals. Centuries ago, Abdul Rahman Ibn Khaldun argued in his *Prolegomena* that people draw their knowledge and ethics, and creeds and virtues, from learning and education, but also from imitation and direct instruction.

## Education and change

Education has been an inherent part of human societies since ancient times. Before the advent of writing, adults would train youths in certain crafts and skills orally, using direct guidance or stories and tales passed down from generation to generation. With the development of societies and urban communities, human knowledge expanded beyond the apprenticeship revolving around crafts and skills, paving the way for institutional education. It is possible the ancient Middle Kingdom of Egypt was a pioneer here, establishing formal schools in the second millennium BC. Then, in the sixth century BC, Confucius founded his doctrine, which had a huge impact on educational systems in the countries of the Far East.

In the following century, Plato founded his academy in Athens. Plato's academy is considered the first institution of higher education in the Western world. Alexandria then succeeded Athens, with its renowned library and sciences, from mathematics to philosophy and literature.

In the Middle Ages, education proliferated in the Arab and Muslim realms. At first, this was linked to the mosque, but then education soon had its own space in the *madrasa*, Arabic for school.

The *madrasas* had a distinctive approach to education, and were centres of intellectual and educational enlightenment not only in the religious sciences, but also in other useful sciences, combining theory and practice, ethical and utilitarian knowledge and worldly and spiritual matters.

Indeed, the *madrasas* taught mathematics, astronomy, astrology, geography, alchemy and philosophy. They fuelled a growth in literacy across the Muslim world in the Middle Ages, with literacy rates comparable to those in Athens in antiquity.

One problem with these schools, however, was that they were not connected by a rigorous institutional system. Instead, they were linked to charitable endowments, private estates and persons and religious orders.

Traditional schools in the Arab–Muslim world gradually became a faint memory, as modern education took over. Only a small number of *madrasas* survive, as cultural relics that shrivelled and dried, after failing to keep pace with useful new knowledge and to accommodate modernity. By contrast, modern schools spread in the form that prevailed in the West, particularly in France in the nineteenth century following the French parliament's adoption of the Jules Ferry law on universal education, which became compulsory in 1956.

What matters here is not so much the history, but, rather, the purpose of education as a path to refinement and enlightenment for the individual and the community. Education empowers people and opens the doors to freedom for them, and provides communities with models for coexistence based on cooperation, solidarity, peace and a joint future.

Relevant in this discussion is the Teaching and Learning for a Sustainable Future (TLSF) project launched by UNESCO at the start of the new millennium. One of the experts the international organisation consulted was French philosopher Edgar Morin, who published for the occasion a book titled *Seven Complex Lessons in Education for the Future*.[49]

Morin stresses the need to pay attention to the shortcomings in knowledge caused by error and delusions. Knowledge needs constant redefining, and there is no knowledge ready for consumption. Morin, therefore, recommends an approach to knowledge that would cover basic and comprehensive issues, while integrating partial and local knowledge so that education is not fragmented.

Morin further argues for the need to teach about the human condition. Humans are physiological, biological, psychological, cultural, social and historical beings at the same time. Nevertheless, this compound unity, distinctive of human nature, is totally fragmented by the educational system through its curricula of study. It is essential that every person realises the compound nature of his identity as well as the shared traits with other fellow human beings.

The French philosopher advocates to recognise the unity and compound nature of humans by grouping the knowledge that is dispersed today in natural and human sciences, literature and philosophy, and by underlining that everlasting relationship between unity and diversity in everything that is human.

Morin proposes teaching an Earth identity highlighting the collective destiny of all humans. At the same time, he calls for teaching Earth history – which began with all continents becoming linked together in the early sixteenth century when new continents were discovered.

Yet highlighting our shared destiny should not mean ignoring oppression, dominance and colonialism that plagued and still plague human history. It means emphasising that all humanity faces the same life and death situations, and has a shared destiny.

Morin's fifth lesson is that everything that is uncertain must also be addressed. Morin recommends teaching those uncertain and undefined issues with the same precision found in hard sciences such as physics and biology. He wants people to be taught strategies to confront fluctuations and uncertainty – so that students can learn how to swim in an ocean of uncertainties with the help of an archipelago of certainties.

Morin calls for teaching understanding and accord, as both a means and an end, saying that mutual understanding is a life necessity. Meanwhile, he calls for studying the root causes of the lack of understanding. He argues that studying matters like racial discrimination and xenophobia build solid foundations for education for peace.

Morin also strongly advocates the teaching of ethics. He says that honest ethical relations require mutual monitoring among the individual, the community and the entire human race, something that is possible through democracy. This is what may be termed in the twenty-first century as international solidarity, which is possible through global citizenship, because the whole Earth has become in effect a global homeland.

## Education and Freedom

It might be redundant to recall that educational institutions are among the greatest institutions devised by human civilisation. However, many communities and nations, under various pretexts, no longer give education the attention, funding and sacrifices it deserves. In doing so, they have forgotten the close links between education and freedom, science and progress, schools and development.

The school does not reflect – except in small measure – the ideas, habits and inherited behaviours existing within a community. To me, its genius and worth stem from the fact that it is a tremendous force for change and a laboratory for manufacturing the future.

A good education builds a micro society that embodies the features, values, ethics, skills and harmonious perceptions of the desired macro society. When students leave school or college and enter other social institutions, especially the household, they take with them, consciously or unconsciously, the values and behaviours they have learned, and thus influence their social surroundings.

When I read articles and reports on the state of education in developed nations or Arab countries, I often notice that educational institutions are witnessing a profound crisis in varying degrees in different countries. In my belief, the crisis is the result of the complexity of modern life and the continuous revision of the function of various social institutions. Technological progress, universal access to knowledge and the possibilities for self-learning seem only to have made the crisis of educational institutions worse.

All one has to do is go online to see how information, knowledge and ideas almost overflow from the computer or smartphone screen, at the push of a button. Experts have thus started to question the role and future of the educational institution in the context of modern institutions, though they have found no alternative.

What this means is that revising perceptions about education and thinking about the problems facing it will be worthwhile in order to redefine these institutions. They and their curricula and approaches need to be streamlined to maintain their edge and ability to lead society, without reflecting necessarily the difficulties, obstacles and weaknesses in society such as violence, racism and drug use.

The pioneering position of the educational society stems from its ability to overcome this and hold on to ethics and basic principles. Modern technology might enable easier access to knowledge, but it cannot do much to produce civil humans. Some values cannot be imparted and some skills cannot be learned except through the warmth of human encounter between teacher and pupil. For this reason, the educational institution, despite its crisis, will remain the basic incubator for young people to develop their personality and learn the rules of coexistence.

Education in my view should emphasise tolerance, refinement and enlightenment. It should seek to help young people to go beyond instinct and natural capability, by developing their skills and talents to be able to change themselves and reform their society to be prosperous, upstanding and harmonious. The Quran reminds us 'God does not change the condition of a people until they change what is in themselves'[50], and the instrument of bringing about this change is education and the educational institution.

Perhaps one fundamental shift in modern education is that it is now built on freedom. This supreme value is now a determinant of educational work, its goal being to hone the independence of the individual. This is not just linked to the individualistic tendency in today's world, but also to the drive for coexistence, cooperation and dialogue, for this requires that the learner be a self-sufficient entity who is confident yet aware of his capabilities and limits. Such an individual will be armed with the skills of argument and debate, solving problems and developing opinions rationally.

Individual freedom and independence are paths to the emergence of a democratic society. More importantly, individual freedom provides immunity for societies and nations based on the convergence of the individual wills of citizens who cooperate to solve problems and respect laws.

In this sense, education facilitates and encourages the integration of individuals into their society, as long as they have an open mind and a conscience equipped with faculties like aesthetic appreciation, goodwill, noble values and principles of citizenship and human rights. In turn, all this motivates individuals to take part in building their homeland out of loyalty and the drive to improve it and propel it forward.

# Education in my country

I feel proud that my country has promoted education and knowledge among children, so that they may be up to the standards of our time and its breathtakingly expanding knowledge, in close connection with its technological base and intellectual, social and humanitarian principles that represent the major global trends. We are seeing the social transformation in Qatar bear fruit every day, as part of a rational path and a clear plan.

I cite here one very clear and unequivocal example that also makes me proud: the empowerment of girls and young women in schools and universities. Education has freed their potentials, and allowed them to acquire the skills needed to break into different areas of life.

Today, women are an essential component of progress and development in Qatar. Schools and universities have helped end their erstwhile exclusion and fulfilled for them a key part of their human identity, elevating them to become genuine partners of men, and clearing the road to equality in citizenship, rights and duties.

Many believe that state policies reflect existing social, economic and cultural conditions and structures, and therefore are agents that perpetuate the status quo. However, many facts prove otherwise.

Reality bears witness that the modern state is actually mandated to work to change the status quo, if it wants to be truly modern and part of history. This is especially true with states governing rigid societies created by centuries of stagnation in intellectual and social life and disconnection from the world. In this case, it is the duty of the state to be a main actor in social change, for example through legislation and policies aimed at liberating their citizens and encouraging them to be active participants in their affairs.

Empowering women and giving them the opportunity to learn are examples of the role of the state in my country in effecting social change, with a view to joining modernity and interacting with human progress at large.

Education in general in Qatar and education of women in particular are a source of pride. They are strong evidence that optimism about the future is not an illusion or a false hope, but rather, is firmly based on the perseverance and diligence of our daughters and women leaders. Woman is the future of man, as the French poet Louis Aragon said. Women are the mothers, daughters, sisters and wives, and deserve all love and respect, including in rights and duties.

## Read!

'Read!' declaims the opening verse of the Quran, the first instruction to humankind. Interestingly, in the Arabic dialect of the Maghreb, the word 'read' has a double meaning: to read and also to learn, and, indeed, I believe the first word of the divine revelation meant much more than its literal sense, and had connotations regarding knowledge and learning in general.

An Arab proverb urges us to 'seek knowledge from the cradle to the grave'. Ibn Muflih, in his book *Islamic Etiquette*, narrates the story of a man who noticed that an imam carried an inkwell with him. The man asked: 'O Abu Abdullah, you have already reached [a great] rank and you are the imam of the Muslims, yet you carry with you an inkwell?' Abu Abdullah replied: 'And I shall carry the inkwell to the grave.'

I was raised in a culture that does not understand education to be limited to the attainment of degrees, no matter how vaunted those degrees are and how much they help one find employment. Education in our culture and tradition is a duty for all those who want to follow the path of truth, and an endless sea in whose waters we should cleanse ourselves for as long as we live. I believe that seeking knowledge is akin to the dynamism of life in its progress and decline, or the sea in its ebb and flow. We elevate ourselves and increase the value of our symbolic capital by reading and learning, and we retreat and impoverish ourselves by being content with what we already know.

Here, I feel amazement if not confusion by the relationship many people have – or lack – with books. When I travel, I take with me a book to keep me company and give me some benefit in my idle time. Oddly, many travellers seem to prefer to spend their trips, even on long-haul flights, staring into the void and just killing time.

Similarly, reading is almost absent altogether in our coffee shops and on our public transport, unlike what I have seen in Western capitals. I admit that all our efforts at the Ministry of Culture to encourage reading achieved less than the desired results. When I think about it now I remember the adage 'Education at a young age is like carving on stones'. Once again, this emphasises the role of the educational institution in this matter as well.

A day without reading is worse than the day before it or at best exactly the same. By contrast, a day spent reading is indeed a new day, with new meanings, ideas and emotions learned and developed. I can only understand continuous lifelong learning in this manner and for me it is the rationale of our existence.

Fate dictated that I should serve as an ambassador for my country when I was twenty years old, after obtaining my university degree. However, this early entry into the world of diplomacy was in itself an incentive for me to develop my skills. As soon as I set foot in Damascus, where I served as ambassador between 1974 and 1979, I enrolled in a master's degree programme at the University of Saint Joseph in Lebanon.

The desire to learn and not to be content with my degree helped me greatly in reconciling my diplomatic career in that sensitive period in the history of the Arab Mashreq and Syria, with working hard on a dissertation that I hoped would make the prestigious university and myself proud. This was a personal challenge; my original training limited me to one language, Arabic, although the glorious history and culture of Al-Azhar University and Cairo opened new horizons for me; my only regret is that the young man I was could not have fully benefited from it all in the brief period I spent in Egypt.

I had felt a bit apprehensive when I was appointed ambassador shortly after graduating from university. I was not daunted by the responsibility entrusted to me and what it required in terms of adapting to developments in an area in crisis. I was young and liked to take on challenges and difficulties. No, I was apprehensive my work could take me away from studying, and from my dream to learn more. From a young age, I had a vague dream about attaining the highest levels of knowledge; I knew for certain that it was something very important and that people should not seek it unless they were serious and hardworking, and desired to work for the good of humankind. That vague thing turned out to be a doctorate degree.

This is how my story began with the master's programme in Lebanon. But there was something else even more important, without which I would not be able to fulfil my aspirations: I could not go into modern research and learning with only one language, as much as I am fond of it and take pride in it as the essence of my culture and identity. I thus decided to learn English.

It was a clear and urgent decision and diplomats must not hesitate when issues are this apparent. I thus set out to learn the language of Shakespeare, or, more aptly, the language of his forebears, which is easier to understand.

To be frank, my relationship with language learning has always been one of urgency and determination, away from procrastination, wishful thinking and hesitance. I remember in this regard meeting with our chargé d'affaires at Qatar's embassy in Paris, Mr Yasser al-Mslallim, when I took over as ambassador in 1979 in the Land of Demons and Angels, to borrow from Taha Hussein.

The chargé d'affaires was fairly fluent in French. This was a Thursday. I told him: 'I want to learn French!' I don't remember how exactly he took my request. He might have seen it as a rushed affair, or thought I wanted to learn French so I could converse with the French. I remember him answering politely: 'Let's look into it next week. We will find a good institute.' But I replied clearly and decisively: 'I am going tomorrow! If I don't start tomorrow I will never start.'

And so I started.

In truth, learning French was not about my diplomatic work. My English had improved by then, and I did not have difficulty conversing in it, and in reality it was the lingua franca of diplomacy all around the world. Our French friends were aware it was our second language in the Gulf.

The second top man in the embassy was not aware that my ultimate purpose was to be able to enrol at the l'Université Paris-Sorbonne (Paris IV). My youthful enthusiasm fuelled my passion for knowledge. Praise be to God, this passion has not faded, and it is thanks to it that I am still enthusiastic about reading and writing.

Nevertheless, my decision to learn French quickly was very useful in my career, and brought almost immediate rewards. A month later, I had to present my Letter of Credence to President Giscard d'Estaing. Mr Merimée, his head of protocol, asked me if I needed an interpreter. I said yes, believing the meeting would proceed in Arabic and French.

The day came. I waited in a room close to the president's office. Suddenly, Mr Merimée came in, visibly embarrassed. The interpreter was late and he did not know what to do. I told him: 'Don't worry, I will manage!' I saw his face take on an expression of astonishment; he knew, I did not speak French but I repeated what I said and went in.

What Mr Merimée did not know is that, days before the meeting, I had asked my language school to rehearse a scenario in which I had to meet with the president without an interpreter. We prepared the phrases we should use in these meetings, which usually do not last more than ten minutes, and I memorised them. I had enough vocabulary and sentences to fill those ten minutes, although my pronunciation was wanting.

My Plan B worked. President Giscard d'Estaing was pleasantly surprised because I went to the effort of addressing him in his own language. He ignored my mistakes, and we would have an excellent relationship thereafter. The head of protocol was also very pleased, and remained grateful for the favour I did him, for the duration of my mission in France. I thus learned that dealing with people in their own language brings us closer and is a source of mutual appreciation and respect.

When the necessities of diplomatic work took me to New York, my enthusiasm did not abate. Working as ambassador to the United Nations was not easy, but I took the risk and enrolled in a PhD programme at the State University of New York in 1984, finishing in 1990.

I cannot hide my pride in this degree, for having helped me discover that vague thing and finally made it clear. When the grown-up man discovered the meaning of the doctorate, he was able to explain to the child and young man he had been what had been hard for them to understand.

I remember, as I recall that distant past, that after I submitted and presented my thesis, I felt as if I was entering a new phase full of work and diligence. I had a strong desire to write and communicate with people. By virtue of my work at the time, only journalistic writing offered me a space to express my views and interact with readers.

In truth, contemplating my personal experience has revealed to me two things I would like to share with the readers. Although I reached a senior position at an early age that others may find grand enough to focus on exclusively, I felt – and this is not false modesty on my part at all – that the post fate brought me was bigger than me and that I did not deserve it unless I expanded my knowledge and expertise.

Those who occupy a post should be up to its rank, so that they may serve in it confidently and perform their duties to the fullest, and serve their country that put its trust in them to protect its interest and promote it among nations. To me, and this is something I firmly believe in, 'the free hold themselves to account'.

At the same time, I see in my own character constant tension caused by my perfectionism. As soon as I finish a job I feel I could have done it better. For example, when I wrote for newspapers I would ask the editor to send the article back quickly so I could revise and edit before sending it for publication.

For me, a person must seek perfection in everything even if this is impossible to achieve. The principle of overcoming barriers is crucial for me, so that every one of us can give others the best thing he has.

Diligence in intellect and work for the sake of humanity is our calling. The quest for perfection elevates us and helps us overcome difficulty, and become beacons and guiding lights for humankind.

## Education above all

My pride in Qatar's investment in education as the key to unlocking potential and changing people and society grows twofold when I find that it has gone beyond Qatari citizens to help shape global citizens in different ways. This is an international and human dimension that is familiar to those working in global education issues, and one that Qatar is working hard to quietly promote.

Qatar profoundly believes that global peace can only be achieved in the context of genuine international solidarity where all children of the world have equal access to education wherever they may be. We are working quietly toward this goal because we seek neither self-promotion nor public rewards and gratitude. There could be children in the world who are denied the chance of enrolling in schools but who are potential geniuses who can benefit all of humankind.

Beyond the logic of narrow interests and international prestige, our educational preoccupations are no longer limited to our citizens, but have gone beyond to the world at large through international programmes with direct and tangible influence on individuals, families and societies in many countries.

As is known, talent is equally distributed among people, but unfortunately the same cannot be said about access to education and talent development. UNESCO has realised that change must first happen in minds, and that the instrument with which this may be achieved is education. Therefore, it is the responsibility of nations and peoples to make education accessible to all, to help humanity develop and improve its capacity in the hope of fulfilling its dreams and aspirations. This can only be achieved by changing minds to build the desired peace, in hearts and consciences first and foremost.

As part of this realistic diagnosis but idealistic outlook, I must say that I admire what my country is doing in education. I have been particularly impressed by two initiatives launched by the State of Qatar, which had a profound impact far from the peninsula's borders: Education Above All and the World Innovation Summit for Education (WISE). Both initiatives are the brainchildren of Her Highness Sheikha Moza bint Nasser, wife of the Father Emir. Sheikha Moza is also behind the Qatar Foundation for Education, Science and Community Development, an organisation with few counterparts in the world, which has attracted world-class universities and talents to serve as a beacon in the Gulf region and beyond.

This exceptional woman serves as a shining example of the enlightened Arab woman. She is a pioneer of modernisation and enlightenment in Qatari and Arab society, and is working hard to empower women and develop society through education and research. Education Above All is an international initiative launched in 2012 and overseen by Sheikha Moza. Its goal is to build an international movement that can contribute to human, social and economic development by providing quality education and other welfare programmes and initiatives. The Education Above All foundation is an umbrella for three programmes: Educate a Child; Al Fakhoora; and Protecting Education in Insecurity and Armed Conflict. These programmes provide an opportunity to those who are denied education to enjoy its fruits and privileges.

Perhaps the most important characteristic of this international humanitarian effort is that the foundation focuses particularly on areas suffering from poverty, conflict and disasters. The foundation seeks to empower children, youth and women to be active members of their communities. By providing them with education, the foundation's role is to supply them with the instruments to achieve sustainable development and to build a culture of peace, justice and prosperity.

The rationale of the foundation is consistent with what we previously outlined, namely that education is the key to social change, progress and freedom.

Since education is both a service and a human right inseparable from its social context, the foundation, in addition to its services in primary education, school enrolment and higher education, covers other issues including healthcare and basic rights. These various efforts support human development and at the same time provide people in need the opportunity to build a better future.

In the first six months of its work, the foundation managed to help half a million children enrol in schools. By the end of 2015, five million children are expected to have enrolled through the foundation in the Middle East, Africa and Latin America – as the foundation covers 120 countries.

The international community has pledged since the end of the twentieth century not to leave any child without basic education within fifteen years of the start of the new millennium. However, the latest statistics on education published by UNESCO in 2014 indicate there are fifty-eight million children in the world still not at school. This means the international community must continue its efforts after the end of the Millennium Development Goals (MDGs) of the United Nations and its agencies.

Her Highness Sheikha Moza expressed it clearly when she said, 'As the MDGs expire in December 2015, we must not break our promise to provide basic education for all. We will seek to ensure that the fifty-eight million children that schools did not open their doors to are not forgotten in the post-2015 development framework.'[51]

## World Innovation Summit for Education (WISE)

Qatar's commitment before the international community is clear with initiatives such as WISE. WISE is an initiative launched by the Qatar Foundation to contribute to the future of education in the world through innovation and empowering the less fortunate to benefit from the best practices in education. WISE also focuses on improving educational instruments, processes and best practices as it is not enough just to provide universal education, particularly in poor and marginalised areas.

WISE convenes once a year in Doha, in a meeting attended by more than 1,500 experts in education and governance, and from the private sector and NGOs. The summit lasts three days and features a large number of workshops, panel discussions and brainstorming sessions. It is also an opportunity to highlight success stories in education.

The conference offers inducements and prizes to encourage all stakeholders, from students to political decision makers. WISE also highlights their pioneering projects and distinguished achievements in education globally.

Some participants have shared moving stories about the impact of education in their lives and communities. One such story was told by Suad Sharif Mohammad, a teacher refugee at the Kakuma refugee camp in Kenya. She said, 'When I was in the second year in primary school my father wanted to marry me off because he needed the dowry from my fiancé's family. But my mother was a great woman and understood the value of education in our lives. I told my father: "What you would get is just a dowry. Let me finish studying and I will bring you more money than you would get from my dowry."'

With her father's permission, and with the help of the Kakuma programme for Education Above All and the UNHCR, Suad finished school, went to university and graduated with a degree in education. Today, Suad is a role model for young women and young men around the world who recognise that education can change lives for the better.

The WISE prize, which is supervised by the initiative itself, has helped improve the quality of education and raise awareness of the importance of education as part of a global agenda. Many international media consider this prize the equivalent of a Nobel Prize in Education. Over the years, the WISE initiative has succeeded in creating global ambassadors who defend education all around the world, and a network of pioneers inspiring future generations and working to bring about change in the service of educational issues.

# Chapter Nine
# The Creative Industries

A summit of the thirteenth UN Conference on Trade and Development (UNCTAD) was convening for the first time in the Gulf in 2012. It was expected that the presidency of the country nominated by the host would extend through to 2017.

This is something that diplomats and others who follow UNCTAD events are no doubt aware of. However, there are details from behind the scenes that people do not know, and I would like to share one of these stories, which is both amusing and relevant.

The host country nominated its minister of culture, arts and heritage to preside over the conference. This came as a surprise to the officials of the organisation, which deals with issues of trade and development. It may even have been seen as a mistake or a poor choice.

One can only imagine the embarrassment the preparatory committee in the international organisation must have felt after the nomination. It was a crisis that needed to be dealt with delicately; diplomatic norms granting the host country the right to choose the president of the conference had to be respected, but an important matter such as the presidency could not be compromised.

What relationship, after all, was there between culture and trade, and art and development? Even if we agree that they are linked, albeit indirectly, would this candidate, who apparently knew little about trade and its specific language, be able to oversee a conference with so much at stake? The presidency must fulfil major international requirements, and requires shrewdness and diplomatic skill in managing multilateral talks and helping bring viewpoints closer together on extremely sensitive matters.

In short, how could a minister of culture, no matter how experienced, head a conference on trade?

There was no solution except for the preparatory committee to ask the Gulf nation to verify its choice. But the Gulf nation's response came quickly: Yes, we are certain about our choice and here is his curriculum vitae.

In truth, I do not know what kind of discussion took place between the UN officials, but they must soon have realised that the candidate was one of their own, a veteran of the leading schools of multilateral diplomacy, that is the United Nations and UNESCO.

The candidate's CV showed him to have served as his country's permanent envoy to UNESCO and as ambassador in Paris. He then became his country's ambassador to the United Nations in New York, a capacity in which he served for six years. Yet, what was most important in his track record was not knowledge of the United Nations and two of its specialised agencies, but, rather, his experience with the overlap between politics, the economy and social and legal issues.

The matter was settled. It was clear the candidate was very suitable. All surprise and confusion vanished, and everyone was reassured.

I forgot to mention something: the country that organised the thirteenth UNCTAD summit was none other than my country, Qatar, and the minister of culture, arts and heritage who was nominated to preside over it was none other than yours truly.

My diplomatic and political experience showed me clearly the profound link between culture and creativity, and tangible and intangible human development. Culture is the foundation that gives development its ethical orientation and reaffirms its social responsibility, rather than being another domain for development that complements the rest.

The UNCTAD was an opportunity to emphasise my views in this regard. I have made this a staple item on the agenda that I have stressed on many occasions. I recall before that that I had said on the occasion of the International Year for the Culture of Peace (1999):

> *Taking advantage of culture and creativity ... to serve peace and deepen human connections among nations requires creating a social, economic and political reality based on justice and equality. Indeed, peace is a strategic and noble goal sought by nations, and war and violence are an exception imposed on nations ... For this reason, it is the duty of the United Nations and its organisations, including UNESCO, which is concerned with science, culture and education, to work to remove obstacles hindering peace. They must remove or at least reduce the informational and economic gap between the rich Global North and the poor Global South, remove weapons of mass destruction (WMDs) from all countries without exception, prevent pollution and preserve the environment. [They must seek to] remove injustice and aggression, restore rights, promote respect for the sanctities of nations and peoples and launch dialogue between civilisations based on justice and mutual respect. These are some of the efforts needed to promote the values of peace and friendship among cultures, including the Arab culture. Resisting violence and wars cannot be done by cursing them, but by removing their causes.*[52]

## Creative industries

Global trade in creative goods and services totalled a record of US $624 billion in 2011 and more than doubled from 2002 to 2011. At the same time, creativity and culture have a significant non-monetary value that contributes to inclusive social development, to dialogue and understanding between peoples.[53]

This is the main message of the Special Edition of the United Nations Creative Economy Report, *Widening Local Development*

163

*Pathways*[54], jointly published in 2013 by UNESCO and the United Nations Development Program (UNDP) through the UN Office for South-South Cooperation. The report was a major contribution to shaping a new and bold sustainable development agenda to follow 2015 that recognises the power of culture as an enabler and a driver.

The creative economy – which includes audiovisual products, design, new media, performing arts, publishing and visual arts – is not only one of the most rapidly growing sectors of the world economy, it is also a highly transformative one in terms of income generation, job creation and export earnings. Between 2002 and 2011, developing countries averaged 12.1 per cent annual growth in exports of creative goods.

'While creating jobs, creative economy contributes to the overall wellbeing of communities, individual self-esteem and quality of life, thus achieving inclusive and sustainable development. At a time when the world is shaping a new post-2015 global development agenda, we must recognise the importance and power of the cultural and creative sectors as engines of that development', said Irina Bokova, Director-General of UNESCO.

The report builds on examples that demonstrate how the creative economy is diverse and innovative, enhancing lives and livelihoods at the local level in developing countries. The cultural and creative industries in Argentina, for example, employ some 300,000 people and represent 3.5 per cent of the country's GDP. In Morocco, publishing and printing employ 1.8 per cent of the labour force, with a turnover of more than US $370 million. The market value of the music industry was more than US $54 million in 2009 and has increased steadily since. In Bangkok, Thailand, there are over 20,000 businesses in the fashion industry alone, while across the region young people are earning a living as small-scale designers.

In the city of Pikine, Senegal, the association Africulturban has created the Hip Hop Akademy, which trains local young people in digital graphics and design, music and video production, promotional management and marketing, as well as D Jing, and English. This innovative programme is helping young creative industry professionals perform more effectively in both a local and global market that is in perpetual artistic and technological evolution.

In Chiang Mai, in northern Thailand, the Chiang Mai Creative City (CMCC) initiative, a think-tank cum activity and networking platform, has been launched as a cooperative endeavour by activists from the education, private and government sectors as well as local community groups. Building upon all of the cultural assets available locally, the CMCC aims to make the city more attractive as a place to live, work and invest in, while marketing it as a prime location for investment, businesses and creative industries. The report also features case studies about the Nigerian film industry (Nollywood), the development of home textile industry in Nantong (China) and the City of Buenos Aires support to content producers, among other examples.

The report puts forward ten key recommendations with a view to forging new cultural pathways to development:

1. *Recognise that in addition to its economic benefits the creative economy also generates non-monetary value that contributes significantly to achieving people-centred, inclusive and sustainable development*

2. *Make culture a driver and enabler of economic, social and environmental development processes*

3. *Reveal opportunities through mapping local assets of the creative economy*

4. *Strengthen the evidence base through rigorous data collection as a fundamental upstream investment to any coherent creative economy development policy*

5. *Investigate the connections between the informal and formal sectors as crucial for informed creative economy policy development*

6. *Analyse the critical success factors that contribute to forging new pathways for local creative economy development*

7. *Invest in sustainable creative enterprise development across the value chain*

165

8. *Invest in local capacity-building to empower creators and cultural entrepreneurs, government officials and private sector companies*
9. *Engage in South-South cooperation to facilitate productive mutual learning and inform international policy agendas for development*
10. *Mainstream culture into local economic and social development programmes, even when faced with competing priorities*[55]

# The emergence of the concept of cultural industries

After the Second World War, cultural phenomena geared towards the general public emerged, but they were not all necessarily characterised by quality. It was, therefore, not surprising that criticisms were voiced claiming they debased fine arts, promoted passiveness and shocked the public taste.

At the time, the term 'cultural industry' emerged as a pejorative expression mocking the populist aspect of modern cultural life. The aim of using the word 'industry' right next to 'culture' was to induce a shock amid the heated discussions on the issue. Indeed, industry is something seen as a repetitive, mechanical process, while culture usually has the quality of refinement and creativity.

We should recall that the notion emerged at a time when the modern industrialised lifestyle was coming under fire because of the perceived negative impact of technology and machinery on people's humanity – roughly ten years after Charlie Chaplin's silent film *Modern Times*.[56] The film remains the best satire of machinery and its dominance on human consciousness and the pace of human life.

In the present time, there are divergent views and attitudes regarding cultural industry. On the one hand, the term captures the bipolarity in society between elite culture and popular culture – fine arts versus commercial entertainment. On the other hand, a concept spread among the majority saying that cultural industries are simply those industries that produce cultural goods and services of various kinds, levels and degrees of quality.

For instance, UNESCO defines cultural industries as those industries that 'combine the creation, production and commercialisation of contents which are intangible and cultural in nature. These contents are typically protected by copyright and they can take the form of goods or services.' The special characteristic of these industries is that they are 'central in promoting and maintaining cultural diversity and in ensuring democratic access to culture'. In other words, cultural industries have a dual economic and cultural nature.[57]

## What is creativity and what are the creative industries[58]?

There is no consensus even among psychologists on whether creativity is a special trait exclusive to talented people, or whether it is available to all, with everyone more or less able to produce innovative ideas through learnable techniques and processes.

But if we turn to the modern context, we can classify creativity under three broad categories: cultural and artistic creativity; economic creativity; and scientific and technological creativity. Experts suggest different definitions for each:

Artistic creativity involves imagination and a capacity to generate original ideas and novel ways of interpreting the world, expressed in text, sound and image. Economic creativity is a dynamic process leading towards innovation in technology, business practices, marketing, etc., and is closely linked to gaining competitive advantages in the economy. Scientific creativity involves curiosity and a willingness to experiment and make new connections in problem solving. All of the above involve technological creativity to a greater or lesser extent and are interrelated.

In light of the available literature on the issue of creativity, we may wonder whether there are two different definitions, one continental European and another that is American and Anglo-Saxon. In the first case, creativity is closer to the world of imagination, personal innovation and inspiration in the broad sense. In the second case, it is a process of production and profit, a measurable endeavour particularly when it contributes to economic growth.

Whatever the case, the notion of creative industries captured my attention. A forum held on the sidelines of the thirteenth UNCTAD conference centred around cultural industries. The issue was also discussed by experts during the summit, with the discussions focusing on the importance of cultural industries in development. Outside UNESCO's literature, cultural industries remain the subject of much brainstorming, thinking and analysis, given the novelty of the concept itself.

The term 'creative industries' first appeared in 1994 in Australia, in a report titled *Creative Nation*.[59] The term became more common when the UK government in 1997 created a creative industries task force. The concept expanded to include cultural industries outside arts, and commercial activities that were seen before from a non-economic viewpoint. The high economic importance of creative industries can be seen in official UK data, for example, which put the total worth of these industries in early 2014 at over £71 billion annually.[60]

UNCTAD's definition of the creative industries is that they:

- *are the cycles of creation, production and distribution of goods and services that use creativity and intellectual capital as primary inputs*
- *constitute a set of knowledge-based activities, focused on but not limited to arts, potentially generating revenues from trade and intellectual property rights*
- *comprise tangible products and intangible intellectual or artistic services with creative content, economic value and market objectives*
- *are at the cross-road among the artisan, services and industrial sectors*
- *constitute a new dynamic sector in world trade.*[61]

In addition to these definitions, UNCTAD proposes dividing creative industries into four main categories to facilitate the understanding of the overlap and relations between them[62] with nine sub categories for further clarification.

- *Heritage. Cultural heritage is identified as the origin of all forms of arts and the soul of cultural and creative industries. It is the starting point of this classification. It is heritage that brings together cultural aspects from the historical, anthropological, ethnic, aesthetic and societal viewpoints, influences creativity and is the origin of a number of heritage goods and services as well as cultural activities. Associated with heritage is the concept of 'traditional knowledge and cultural expressions' embedded in the creation of arts and crafts as well as in folklore and traditional cultural festivities. This group is therefore divided into two subgroups:*
    - *Traditional cultural expressions: arts and crafts, festivals and celebrations; and*
    - *Cultural sites: archaeological sites, museums, libraries, exhibitions, etc.*

- *Arts. This group includes creative industries based purely on art and culture. Artwork is inspired by heritage, identity values and symbolic meaning. This group is divided into two large subgroups:*
    - *Visual arts: painting, sculpture, photography and antiques; and*
    - *Performing arts: live music, theatre, dance, opera, circus, puppetry, etc.*

- *Media. This group covers two subgroups of media that produce creative content with the purpose of communicating with large audiences ('new media' is classified separately):*
    - *Publishing and printed media: books, press and other publications; and*
    - *Audiovisuals: film, television, radio and other broadcasting.*

- *Functional creations. This group comprises more demand-driven and services-oriented industries creating goods and services with functional purposes. It is divided into the following subgroups:*
    - *Design: interior, graphic, fashion, jewellery, toys;*
    - *New media: software, video games, and digitalised creative content; and*

*— Creative services: architectural, advertising, cultural and recreational, creative research and development (R&D), digital and other related creative services*[63]

This classification of the creative industries proposed by UNCTAD is exhaustive. The four categories above (i.e. heritage, arts, media and functional creations) cover most human knowledge and its tangible and intangible manifestations. However, we may not agree with the classification of the media, which appears to us artificial or arbitrary.

It is difficult to accept the separation between traditional media and new media, placing the first under 'media' and the second under 'functional creations'. In addition to the fact that traditional media interact organically with new media, which has become the former's arm to access segments traditional media could not reach before, new media itself broadcasts news, talk shows and newspaper content.

We cannot see the new media as merely being a functional creation, as UNCTAD does. For example, social media has gained direct influence on the economy, politics, society and culture in general. The Arab Spring was most probably a product of the new media, which replaced traditional media and the censorship associated with it, as I have argued in this book.

## Creative industries versus cultural industries

The terms 'creative industries' and 'cultural industries' are often used synonymously. We saw how creativity is not limited to culture, but also covers the economy and science, not to mention technology. Cultural products would include products from the arts, literature, and artisan and heritage crafts. Creative industries, however, seem to be bigger in scope, including cultural products as well as fashion design, software and other human products that require a degree of creativity. Therefore, cultural goods and services are a subcategory of creative goods and services.

There is an alternative definition of cultural industries, based on the value they produce or represent. In addition to the commercial value of any commodity that may characterise creative industries, the moral, social and cultural values are also relevant. These could include the aesthetic value or these commodities' contribution to understanding the cultural identity of society. The ability to sense this intangible value is what sets apart cultural industries.

Nevertheless, there are still strong divergences in the research community as well in decision- and policy-making circles regarding the notions of creative and cultural industries.

## The creative economy

Cultural economics seek to apply economic models and analyses to arts, heritage and creative industries. They are concerned with the economic organisation of the cultural sector, and trends among producers, consumers and decision makers in this domain.

It seems as though creative producers themselves are embarrassed by this trend. They do not easily accept that market and economic instruments be used to dissect what is at the heart of human creativity, and what did not emerge to necessarily meet the physical demands of humankind but rather to address humanity's consciousness, intellect and emotions. Again, we will refer to the excellent literature provided by UNCTAD:

'The creative economy is an evolving concept based on creative assets potentially generating economic growth and development

- *It can foster income generation, job creation and export earnings while promoting social inclusion, cultural diversity and human development*
- *It embraces economic, cultural and social aspects interacting with technology, intellectual property and tourism objectives*

- *It is a set of knowledge-based economic activities with a development dimension and cross-cutting linkages at macro and micro levels to the overall economy*
- *It is a feasible development option calling for innovative multidisciplinary policy responses and interministerial action*
- *At the heart of the creative economy are the creative industries'*[64]

The term 'creative economy' appeared in 2001 in John Howkins' book about the relationship between creativity and economics.[65] For Howkins, 'creativity is not new and neither is economics, but what is new is the nature and the extent of the relationship between them and how they combine to create extraordinary value and wealth'.

Since any type of economy requires benchmarks for measuring performance, experts identified five indexes to measure the creative economy: manifestations of the creative economy (outputs and outcomes); structural or institutional capital; human capital; social capital; and cultural capital.[66]

## Creative industries and development

My purpose behind this overview of new overlapping concepts related to creative industries was not to explain my understanding of them. Rather, these concepts, as I explained, are closely linked to culture and development. Most modern economic concepts and theories apply to the creative economy, which develops and grows in the same way other sectors do. It is legitimate, therefore, for organisations such as the United Nations, UNESCO and UNCTAD to take interest in the relationship between the creative economy and development, and to conduct studies to inform policies aiming to serve the interests of all.

UNCTAD's literature alludes to creative cities and creative clusters. Experts believe creativity is in the process of overcoming factors such as geography in terms of competitiveness and attracting investments. The essential factor is human capital, in addition to the indexes we mentioned earlier. Creative clusters, networks and districts are now a key element in the urban context of some cities and communities.

As indicated on its website[67], the Creative Cities Network is currently formed by 69 Members from 32 countries covering seven creative fields: Crafts & Folk Art, Design, Film, Gastronomy, Literature, Music and Media Arts. Among them, for example, we find Edinburgh in Scotland as a UNESCO City of Literature, Bologna in Italy and Seville in Spain as UNESCO Cities of Music, Buenos Aires in Argentina, Montreal in Canada and Berlin in Germany as UNESCO Cities of Design, Santa Fe (NM) in the United States and Aswan in Egypt as UNESCO Cities of Folk Art and Popayan in Colombia as UNESCO City of Gastronomy.

The international dimension of creative industries means they will play a crucial role in shaping the future of culture around the world, in relation to anything from freedom of expression and cultural diversity to economic development. But while globalisation of trade and technology indeed opens up new exciting avenues, it also creates new forms of gaps and inequalities.

The distribution of cultural industries in the world reveals a huge gap between north and south. This needs to be addressed by strengthening local capacities and facilitating access to global markets through new partnerships, upgrading technical skills, controlling piracy and increasing international solidarity in all its forms[68].

Since creativity has become a very powerful force in the modern economy, rich cultural resources, creative assets and the heritage in developing countries must act as engines of development, employment and contribution to the global economy. These also allow developing countries to present their own cultural visions, and to better learn about their identities and present these to the world in the best form. The creative economy increases social cohesion, cultural diversity and human development.

We Arabs urgently need to break into this brave new world and ensure we have everything for our efforts to succeed through human, material and, most importantly, intellectual capital. Creative industries would greatly highlight our heritage and take advantage of the talents of our young people, who yearn to enjoy the fruits of modern technology and openness to cultures.

A chance that all decision-makers as well as civil society should take into consideration!

# Afterword
# The Global *Majlis*

Early Arabic literature is replete with beautiful stories and anecdotes. The best I have read tells the story of a man who arrived in a town famous for its many great scholars and thinkers. He wanted to visit the town's cemetery, which he thought would be similar to the famous Panthéon in Paris.

However, after wandering around what he thought was the cemetery of great people, the man was disappointed to find that most of those buried there had died at a very young age. Gravestones bore the names of infants who had lived only for a day or two. The longest any of them had lived was no more than one week.

The man was confused by what he saw on the gravestones, and his confusion doubled when his friend explained to him that all of them had died at an old age after leading long lives as great scholars. 'We do not calculate a man's life by years and months. The only days that count are those in which a man was truly happy or when he did an act of honour!' the man's friend explained.

It is not about the number of days lived, but, rather, about how greatness was associated with a short life.

The original story may be somewhat different from the version I have told, but the moral of the story is quite similar to that which lingered in my mind. The most important element about it is the questions it raises: what does it mean to live? And how do we evaluate someone's life?

What we leave behind as God's successors on Earth will create the dignity endowed by the Creator throughout history and time. 'We have honoured the children of Adam and carried them over land and sea, blessing them with good things and gracing them with preference over others whom we have created.' (Isra: 70)

Our virtue as human beings lies in our thoughts, knowledge, honour and humanity. Thus, we must spread good and beauty, and build on great meanings and higher values. This is what lingers in my mind from the roots of my faith and the cultural tradition I grew up with, as well as what I have gained by reading different philosophical theories and perceptions.

On this I have based my view of existence and my role in life, and this is what I have spared no effort or energy to explain in this book, where I have introduced some points that I consider essential and others that mark certain milestones in my intellectual journey.

And now, after this journey down memory lane and the pathways of human and cultural issues, I can see the meaning of my life in a better and clearer way.

I cannot deny that I needed a self-examination and a look at my life, which I have lived fully. And as I wrote these pages, I was reflecting upon my own humanity and dignity first and foremost.

Indeed, these chapters were a sort of a rest after fighting every day for my values and principles, and to achieve what I aim for in my country and in the larger world of humanity.

I do not claim that the content of this book is an example to follow or a statement whose truth is final. It is, rather, the result of my wish to share some of my concerns about culture with readers, perhaps to motivate them to formulate their own views with full awareness and complete freedom.

I do not have any lessons or examples to offer. I am merely someone who has worked hard and believed, and thus sought to match his work with his views. If at any point in the book the reader finds a good example to follow, I would be glad, but even a mere conversation will suffice, and I would be happier with an intellectual interaction.

In addition to being a conversation with myself, the previous chapters have been a conversation about several broad ideas, as I hoped to reach a conclusion regarding my intellectual relationship with others. The most I hoped for was to have a conversation with the reader, whom I do not know, because for me writing is an invitation for discussion.

I cannot deny that I found great pleasure and comfort in recalling stories and turning my inner thoughts into words on the page. In some ways, this book can be considered a mirror that reflects parts of my intellectual and professional life, since my positions and responsibilities have allowed me to combine words and action, as well as to experience my own perceptions and thoughts in real life.

Here, I would like to explain two concepts that have become clear to me as I wrote this book. I have seen my own reflection in the mirrors of the previous chapters as an ambitious man who claimed that resolutions are measured against the resolve of those who make them.

The first is my will, which is based on my deep belief in freedom and reason and not on whims or desires, because it is about the necessary ethics. In its deepest meaning, the general interest remained my compass bearing, which kept me on the right track whenever I lost my way.

I believe that choices based on free will are the essence of our human dignity and the way to shape our being grounded in values and ideals. For me, this disproves the false dichotomy between reason and faith, as they both expand our freedom and are both based on the concept of duty. No faith is real without good deeds, and no reason is viable without ethics. When we are able to feel the suffering of others, we are able to help alleviate it and fulfil their dreams.

177

The second is ambition, which is based on the desire to rise towards something better and cross over to the desired goal. But I believe perfection and greatness can only be achieved through tireless work. Ambition is not about lust for power and money by any means possible, under the pretext that the end justifies the means. I believe ambition is a desire for perfection and success and for achieving high aspirations with honour and integrity. It seeks to do good and achieve prosperity, where individual desires unite to benefit the people, who will in turn be forever grateful. 'As for the scum, it goes to be thrown away, while that which benefits people remains on the earth.'[69]

When I saw my reflection through this book as an ambitious man, determination made my task easier. One of the things I know about myself is that if I set my mind to something, I become very disciplined, especially if things are clear. I leave hesitation aside and work hard to achieve my goal. Clarity is a requirement for success, and genuine hard work is a requirement for achievements. Resolutions are measured against the resolve of those who make them.

Thus, when we combine free will with perfection seeking ambition and determination based on good views and hard work, my faith becomes clear to me as does my motto in life: if you yearn for the impossible you will achieve it.

What could we achieve if we rose beyond language, culture, race and belief? What could we realise and learn?

No matter how different and diverse cultures are, one thing is certain: wherever you go, you will find common ground among human beings, who share the same needs, such as food, health and education, or what can be called food for body and thought.

Aleksandr Solzhenitsyn spoke about the trinity of truth, goodness and beauty, which he believed was the foundation of everything that is human.

*So perhaps that ancient trinity of Truth, Goodness and Beauty is not simply an empty, faded formula as we thought in the days of our self-confident, materialistic youth? If the tops of these three trees converge, as the scholars maintained, but the too blatant, too direct stems of Truth and Goodness are crushed, cut down, not allowed through — then perhaps the fantastic, unpredictable, unexpected stems of Beauty will push through and soar to that very same place, and in so doing will fulfil the work of all three?[70]*

Thus, when I considered the issue of localisation and globalisation, I found that inter-cultural dialogue can protect local cultures and enrich common human values away from stereotyping. Traditions protect cultures from being deformed, and opening up to universal modernity waters their lush trees. This proves the need to pay attention to culture-focused development in order to bridge the gaps between local and universal culture, between intellectual and popular culture and between the elite and the public.

The chapter on the aesthetic exploration of the world showed how art and literature were humankind's best creations, communicating and uniting people to fulfil common dreams and build a brighter future. Art and literature are not pointless aesthetic luxuries; they are the outcome of collective dreams, painted by artists and expressed by writers who all believe in the genuine link between beauty, truth, ethics and freedom. Art and literature have the ability to transcend national borders and racial, linguistic and ideological differences. In their essence, art and literature are a discussion and a meeting point for individual and collective dreams.

Despite the changes and issues that undermined prior convictions, as shown by the new media, the public sphere has become richer, expanding the limits of modern humanity and opening up new spaces for freedom, thus bringing back the issues of democracy and its possible forms. The network connecting freedom, democracy, public spheres and media is woven by rational dialogue and discussions about what benefits individuals and groups.

Through different forms of cultural diplomacy, this dialogue has been held among countries, governments, peoples and civil society groups around the world. This dialogue has become established through institutions that organise and develop it, as well as use it to bring people closer together, with the aim of knowing and understanding each other to lay the foundations for peace in hearts and minds.

Another form of seeking this peace appears in the dialogue between politicians and diplomats in international forums for joint discussions about the reality and future of humankind. Cultural diplomacy does not achieve immediate results, since changing mindsets in the long term is a slow process, but multilateral diplomacy in an international political context requires swift decision making, as devastating wars may result from the delay in making such decisions and the rush to secure peace.

However, what makes me look at the world of people with a degree of optimism is the emergence of a form of trans cultural citizenship that represents one aspect of the deep faith in the unity of humankind now and in the future. When a direct encounter between people of different faiths, races and ethnicities is made possible, and when they realise there is no room for them on Earth without understanding, communication and dialogue, a culture of humility, relativity, respect and cooperation begins to prevail.

The spread of education around the world has contributed to this trend of global citizenship. It is the best tool for changing mindsets and societies, as well as investing properly in humanity. Through education, people learn the rules of coexistence and adopting individual and collective identities based on freedom and duty.

In the chapter about creative industries, I wanted to point out some trends of the knowledge economy and the new horizons for investing in human intelligence and creativity. Today, the relationship between economy, knowledge and cultural creativity is more complicated than ever. We cannot overlook this new reality, which has become certain in all successful development models. Cultural industries are an essential part of producing wealth, increasing capital, valuing artistic creativity, developing culture and creating new and promising professions.

However, despite all these global trends that prove the advancement of mankind and the development of intelligence levels and practical applications, we cannot ignore the signs of a return of primitive barbarism, most evident in a 'sacred ignorance' campaign, destroying monuments that were until recently the equivalent of open-air museums. This shows that humankind still has a long way to go before it can protect itself from destruction and obliteration, yet it is destined to take this path despite everything that is happening.

It is no surprise that when man first rose above the ground in a plane, he realised he was looking at the *Terre des Hommes*, the 'Land of men', as described by French aviator and writer Antoine de Saint-Exupéry.

This was in the beginning of the twentieth century and here we are coming to the same realisation in the beginning of the twenty-first century. Will we learn our lesson?

We are all of us aboard the same boat, in the 'Land of men', and we are all citizens of this planet, without exception.

# Arabic works cited

أبو الطيّب المتنبّي، (أحمد بن حسين الجعفي المتنبّي أبو الطيب)، «ديوان المتنبي» (١٩٨٣)، دار بيروت للطباعة والنشر، لبنان.

أبو جعفر محمد بن جرير الطبري، «تاريخ الطبري: تاريخ الأمم والملوك» ٢٠٠٣، دار ومكتبة الهلال، القاهرة.

آمال القرامي، «الاختلاف في الثقافة العربية الإسلامية» (٢٠٠٧)، دار المدار الإسلامي، بيروت.

الأمانة العامة للتخطيط التنموي «استراتيجية التنمية الوطنية لدولة قطر ٢٠١١-٢٠١٦ نحو رؤية قطر الوطنية ٢٠٣٠»، (٢٠١١) الدوحة، قطر.

أنور الخطيب، «السياسة أفسدت الثقافة» (لقاء مع وزير الثقافة القطري)، صحيفة «العربي الجديد» بتاريخ ٢٣ /١١ /٢٠١٤، لندن.

أهداف سويف (تحرير) «تأملات في الفنّ الإسلامي» (٢٠١١)، هيئة متاحف قطر، الدوحة.

بنسالم حمّيش، «العلاّمة» (٢٠١١)، دار الآداب، بيروت.

بنسالم حمّيش، «مجنون الحكم» (٢٠١٢)، دار الشروق، القاهرة.

بنسالم حمّيش، «هذا الأندلسيّ» (٢٠١١)، دار الآداب، بيروت.

جان ماري لوكليزيو، «صحراء» مترجم إلى العربية في «كشف المستور: قراءات نقدية في الأدب العالمي» (٢٠١٠)، الدار العربية للعلوم ناشرون، لبنان. ودار محمد علي تونس. ص: ١٢٢-١٢٣.

جورج طرابيشي، «إشكاليات العقل العربي: نقد نقد العقل العربي» (٢٠٠٢)، دار الساقي، بيروت.

حمد بن عبدالعزيز الكوّاري، «المعرفة الناقصة: العرب والغرب في عالم متغيّر» (٢٠٠٥)، رياض الريس للكتب والنشر، بيروت.

حمد بن عبدالعزيز الكواري، «جدل المعارك والتسويات: الحرب الخليجية الأولى ومجلس الأمن» (٢٠٠١)، دار المستقبل العربي، القاهرة.

«دليل متحف المتروبوليتان للفنون» (٢٠١٤) النسخة العربية، إصدارات متحف المتروبوليتان، نيويورك.

سكوت مونتغوميري، «العلم في الترجمة: حركات المعرفة عبر الثقافات والزمن»، ترجمة إبراهيم الشهابي، مراجعة وفاء التومي (٢٠١٠)، وزارة الثقافة والفنون والتراث، الدوحة، قطر.

سير عنترة وسيف بن ذي يزن والظاهر بيبرس وتغريبة بني هلال.

الصادق الحمامي، «الميديا الجديدة: الإبستيمولوجيا والإشكاليات والسياقات» (٢٠١٢) سلسلة البحوث، المنشورات الجامعية بمنوبة، تونس.

عبدالرحمن بن محمد بن خلدون، «المقدمة»، تحقيق علي عبدالواحد وافي (٢٠٠٦) سلسلة التراث، الهيئة المصرية العامة للكتاب، القاهرة.

عبدالكريم الحيزاوي، «برامج المرأة في الإذاعات العربية» (٢٠٠٤)، اتحاد إذاعات الدول العربية، تونس.

عبدالعزيز المطاوعة، «المجلس والقهوة في شعر الشاعر صالح بن سلطان الكواري» مجلة المأثورات الشعبية، العدد ٦٨ السنة ٢٣، إبريل ٢٠١٤، إدارة التراث، وزارة الثقافة والفنون والتراث، الدوحة، قطر.

عبدالله محمد بن مفلح المقدسي، «الآداب الشرعية» تحقيق شعيب الأرنؤوط وعمر القيام (١٩٩٩) ٣ أجزاء، مؤسسة الرسالة ناشرون، لبنان.

القاضي الرشيد بن الزبير، «كتاب الذخائر والتحف»، تحقيق محمد حميد الله ومراجعة صلاح الدين المنجد (١٩٥٩)، دائرة المطبوعات والنشر، الكويت ص: ٩-١٠.

لوسيان بولاسترون، «كتب تحترق: تاريخ تدمير المكتبات» (٢٠١٠)، ترجمة هاشم صالح ومحمد مخلوف، نشر وزارة الثقافة والفنون والتراث قطر مع الدار العربية للعلوم ناشرون بيروت، ودار محمد علي للنشر، تونس.

مايكل كرونين، «الترجمة والعولمة»، ترجمة محمود منقذ الهاشمي وعبدالودود العمراني، مراجعة حسام الخطيب (٢٠١٠)، الدار العربية للعلوم ناشرون، لبنان. وزارة الثقافة والفنون والتراث، الدوحة، قطر.

«مجلد دليل فعاليات الاحتفالية: الدوحة عاصمة الثقافة العربية ٢٠١٠» (٢٠١١)، وزارة الثقافة والفنون والتراث، الدوحة، قطر.

«محاضرات الحائزين على جائزة نوبل للأدب، الجزء الأول» (٢٠١١)، ترجمة عبدالودود العمراني ومراجعة وفاء التّومي، وزارة الثقافة والفنون والتراث، قطر. الدار العربية للعلوم ناشرون، لبنان، دار محمد علي الحامّي، تونس.

«محاضرات الحائزين على جائزة نوبل للأدب، الجزء الثاني» (٢٠١٢)، ترجمة عبدالودود العمراني ومراجعة وفاء التّومي، وزارة الثقافة والفنون والتراث، قطر. الدار العربية للعلوم ناشرون، لبنان. دار محمد علي الحامّي، تونس.

محمد عابد الجابري، «بنية العقل العربي: دراسة تحليلية نقدية لنظم المعرفة في الثقافة العربية»، مركز دراسات الوحدة العربية، بيروت، طبعات عديدة.

مشهور بن حسن آل سلمان، «إعلام العابد في حكم تكرار الجماعة في المسجد الواحد» (١٤١٢هجري)، الطبعة الثانية، دار المنار، القاهرة.

منصور عبدالحكيم، «سيد ملوك بني العباس هارون الرشيد، الخليفة الذي شُوّه تاريخه عمدًا» (٢٠١١)، دار الكتاب العربي، بيروت، ص: ٢٩٢.

نبيل علي ونادية حجازي، «الفجوة الرقمية» (٢٠٠٥)، سلسلة عالم المعرفة الكويتية، العدد ٣١٨، أغسطس ٢٠٠٥.

نجيب محفوظ، «السكريّة».

نجيب محفوظ، «القاهرة الجديدة».

نجيب محفوظ، «بين القصرين».

نجيب محفوظ، «رادوبيس».

نجيب محفوظ، «عبث الأقدار».

نجيب محفوظ، «قصر الشوق».

نجيب محفوظ، «كفاح طيبة».

# Works Cited

Al-Khalili, Jim, *Pathfinders: The Golden Age of Arabic Science*, UK, Allen Lane, Penguin Books, 2010

Aragon, Louis, *Le Fou d'Elsa: Poésie*, Paris, Gallimard, 2002

*Archives carolingiennes Annales Royales des Francs – De l'année 741 à l'année 829*, Nyon, Editions Paleo, 2001

Baudry, Antonin, *Séminaire sur la diplomatie culturelle: La force de l'autre. A quoi sert la diplomatie culturelle? Disponible (audio) en ligne sur le site de l'ENS*, Paris, 2012

Beulé, Charles Ernest, *Revue des Deux Mondes*, T. 56, Paris, 1865

Bordas, Nicolas, *L'idée qui tue*, Paris, Editions Eyrolles, 2011

Clot, A., *Suleiman the Magnificent: The Man, His Life, His Epoch*, London, Saqi Books, 1992

Cummings, Milton, *Cultural Diplomacy and the United States Government: A Survey, Cultural Diplomacy Research Center for Arts and Culture*, 26 June 2009

Debray, Régis, *Introduction à la médiologie*, Paris, PUF, 2000

Emerson, Ralph Waldo, *Gifts: An Essay*, South Carolina, USA, Bibliolife, 2009

Fuentes, Carlos, *Géographie du roman*, Paris, Essai Gallimard, 1997

Gienow-Hecht, J. C. E and Donfried M. C., *Searching for a Cultural Diplomacy*, New York and Oxford, Bergham Books, 2010

Howkins, John, *The Creative Economy: How People Make Money from Ideas*, UK, Penguin Books (second edition), 2013

Korchilov, Igor, *Translating History: Thirty Years on the Front Lines of Diplomacy with a Top Russian Interpreter*, New York, Simon & Schuster, 1999

Kundera, Milan, *L'insoutenable légèreté de l'être*, Paris, Collection Folio, Paris, Gallimard, 1984

Maalouf, Amin, *Les identités meurtrières*, Paris, Livre de Poche, 2001

Malraux, André, dans le film *La métamorphose du regard* (35 min.), Réalisé par Clovis Prévost, 1973

Morin, Edgar, *Les Sept Savoirs Nécessaires à l'Education du Futur*, UNESCO 1999. Paris, Seuil, 2000

Ovide, *Les Métamorphoses*, Paris, Etonnants Classiques, Flammarion, 2014

Radbourne, Jennifer, 'Creative Nation – A Policy for Leaders or Followers? An Evaluation of Australia's 1994 Cultural Policy Statement', *The Journal of Arts Management, Law and Society*, Vol. 26. Issue 4, 1997, DOI: 10.1080/10632921.1997.9942966, 2010 online

Saint-Exupéry, Antoine de, *Terre des Hommes*, Paris, Folio, Gallimard, 1972

Saint-Exupéry, Antoine de, *Vol de Nuit*, Paris, Folio, Gallimard, 1972

Sfeir-Younis, Alfredo, 'The Role of Civil Society in Foreign Policy: A New Conceptual Framework', *Seton Hall Journal of Diplomacy and International Relations*, Summer/Fall 2004

Shalem, Avinoam, 'Objects as Carriers of Real or Contrived Memories in a Cross-Cultural Context: The Case of the Medieval Diplomatic Presents and Trophies of Wars', Lecture given at the conference 'Migrating Images', Berlin, 2003

A Study on Creativity Index, Home Affairs Bureau and University of Hong Kong, 2005

US Department of State, *Cultural Diplomacy: The Linchpin of Public Diplomacy*, Report of the Advisory Committee on Cultural Diplomacy, Washington, DC, 2005

# Notes

**Introduction**

[1] Le Clézio, J. M., *Desert*., translated from the French by C. Dickson, 2009, David R. Godine, Jaffrey New Hampshire, originally published in French in 1980 as *Désert*, Editions Gallimard, Paris.

**Chapter One**

[2] Montgomery, Scott, *Science in Translation: The Movement of Knowledge Through Cultures and Time*, p. 272, The University of Chicago Press, Chicago and London, 2000.

[3] Ibid., p. 272.

[4] Cronin, Michael, *Translation and Globalization*, p. 97. Routledge, London, 2003

[5] Arab League Mission to the People's Republic of China. 'House of Wisdom in Baghdad Symbol of Dialogue among Civilizations'.

**Chapter Two**

[6] Polastron, Lucien Xavier, *Livres en Feu* (original French title).

[7] See Hamadaaalkawari on Instagram.

[8] Surat al-Hujurat (The Chambers), 13, Yusuf Ali translation, retrieved via www.quranexplorer.com

[9] http://www.louvre.fr/en/missions-projects

[10] *The Metropolitan Museum of Art Guide,* New York, Metropolitan Museum of Art, 2014.

[11] *Ibid.*

¹² http://www.onislam.net/english/culture-and-entertainment/
fine-arts/424707.html

## Chapter Three

¹³ *L'idée qui tue*, Paris, Eyrolles, 2011. The book, originally in
French, has been published in English and is currently being
published in Arabic by the Qatari Ministry of Culture, Arts and
Heritage, 2015.

¹⁴ Qatar, Saudi Arabia and Oman nominated the *majlis* for
the list in 2015. See http://www.unesco.org/culture/
ich/index.php?pg=00704&include=slideshow.inc.
php&id=01076&width=620&call=slideshow&mode = scroll.
For more information about the *majlis* and its roles in the Arab
Gulf nations, see Issue No. 86, April 2014, Ministry of Culture,
Arts and Heritage, Qatar.

¹⁵ 'Politics have ruined culture', Interviewed by Anwar
al-Khatib, 23 November 2014, http://www.alaraby.co.uk/
politics/21fdcfb5-8bfa-40a2-ae12-f07a24fff1c5

¹⁶ Hamad bin Abdulaziz Al-Kawari, Incomplete Knowledge: The
Arabs and the West in a Changing World (Arabic), Beirut, Riad
al-Rayyes Publishing, 2005, pp. 237–8.

¹⁷ Hammami, Sadok, *The New Media: Epistemology, Problems and
Contexts,* Research Series, Tunis, Manouba University Press,
2012.

¹⁸ Ibid., p. 72.

¹⁹ Debray, Régis, *Introduction à la Médiologie*, Paris, PUF, 2000.

²⁰ Hamad bin Abdulaziz Al-Kawari, *Incomplete Knowledge:* pp. 243-
244.

²¹ www.ikono.org

²² Hamadaaalkawari on Instagram.

²³ Hammami, *The New Media.*

## Chapter Four

[24] Including Youssuf Balabbas, Ambassador of Morocco; Taher al-Masri, Ambassador of Jordan; Al-Hadi Mabrouk, Ambassador of Tunisia; Issa al-Hamad, Ambassador of Kuwait; Hamad Al-Kawari, Ambassador of Qatar; Ibrahim al-Sous, Ambassador of Palestine; Youssuf Shakkour, Ambassador of Syria; Jamil Hujailan, Ambassador of Saudi Arabia; Khalifa Al Mubarak, UAE Ambassador; and Ahmed Makki, Ambassador of Oman.

[25] Antonin Baudry delivered a series of lectures in 2012 on cultural diplomacy. His lectures in French can be accessed via this link (06/11/2014): http://savoirs.ens.fr/expose.php?id=650. In addition, Baudry, writing under the pen name Abel Lanzac, wrote the script for the animated film *Quai d'Orsay,* the metonym for the French Foreign Ministry.

[26] Cummings, Milton C., *Cultural Diplomacy and the United States Government: A Survey,* Washington, DC: Center for Arts and Culture. http://www.culturaldiplomacy.org/pdf/case-studies/Hwajung_Kim_Cultural_Diplomacy_as_the_Means_of_Soft_Power_in_the_Information_Age.pdf, 2003.

[27] As mentioned by al-Qazi IBN Al-Zubair in his Al-Zakha'er wal-Tuhaf (The Ammunition and Antiques), one of the most important sources in Islamic heritage, for its narratives, see http://www.iasj.net/iasj?func=fulltext&aId=101639

[28] http://www.bartleby.com

[29] Mentioned in an Arabic medieval book, "Kitab al-Hadaya wa al-Tuhaf" (Book of Gifts and Rarities), edited by M. Hamidullah. The manuscript furnishes a wealth of varied information offering insights into the period immediately preceding Islam and extending through the first four centuries of Islamic rule. The book provides valuable information on "gifts" exchanged on various occasions between Islamic rulers and their foreign counterparts. "Rarities" form a part of the

gifts; some of them are marvels, others are mythical. See: http://www.littlecitybooks.com/book/9780932885135

30 Surat Al-Naml (The Ants), 34-35, Mufti Taqi Usmani translation via http://www.quranexplorer.com

31 Shalem, Avinoam, *Objects as Carriers of Real or Contrived Memories in a Cross-Cultural Context: the Case of the Medieval Diplomatic Presents and Trophies,* http://netzspannung.org/cat/servlet CatServlet?cmd=netzkollektor&subCommand=showEntry&entryId=120311&lang=en

32 Harun al-Rashid, *The Caliph Who Was Smeared by History,* Beirut, Dar al-Kitab al-Arabi, 2011, p. 292.

33 Gienow-Hecht, Jessica C. E., and Donfried, Mark C., *Searching for a Cultural Diplomacy*, New York and Oxford, Berghahn Books, 2010.

34 Ibid.

35 Ibid.

36 Ibid, pp. 24–5.

## Chapter Five

37 Al-Kawari, Hamad bin Abdulaziz, *Incomplete Knowledge: The Arabs and the West in a Changing World* (Arabic), Beirut, Riad al-Rayyes Publishing, pp. 237–8, 2005.

38 Dag Hammarskjöld was killed in a plane crash en route to negotiate a cease-fire on 18 September, 1961 in present-day Zambia. The circumstances of the incident are still not clear. There is some recent evidence that suggest the plane was shot down.

39 G.R Berridge, *Return to the UN: UN Diplomacy in Regional Conflicts,* New York, St Martin's Press 1991.

40 Ibid., pp. 88–93.

41 Korchilov, Igor, *Translating History: Thirty Years on the Front Lines of Diplomacy with a Top Russian Interpreter,* New York, Simon & Schuster, 1999.

[42] http://www.upworthy.com/a-15-year-old-ad-about-racism-is-a-great-reminder-of-the-power-we-all-have-to-promote-justice.

## Chapter Six

[43] http://www.unesco.org/new/en/brasilia/about-this-office/prizes-and-celebrations/international-decade-for-a-culture-of-peace-and-non-violence-for-the-children-of-the-world/

[44] Maalouf, Amin, *Les identités meurtrières*, Paris, Livre de Poche, 2001.

[45] Mohammad Abed al-Jabiri, *The Structure of the Arab Mind*, Center for Arab Unity Studies.

[46] Tarabishi, George, *Problems of the 'Arab Mind'*, Dar al-Saqi.

[47] Surat al-Hujurat (The Chambers), 13, Yusuf Ali translation, retrieved via www.quranexplorer.com

[48] Al-Qarami, Amal, *Differences in the Arab-Islamic Culture*, Dar al-Madar al-Islami, 2007.

## Chapter Seven

[49] Morin, Edgar, *Les Sept Savoirs Nécessaires à l'Education du Futur*, UNESCO 1999, Paris, Seuil, 2000.

[50] Surat Al-Raad (Thunder), 11. Mufti Taqi Usmani translation via http://www.quranexplorer.com

[51] *Education for All* annual report, Doha, 2014.

## Chapter Eight

[52] Al-Kawari, *Incomplete Knowledge*, pp. 289–90.

[53] Creative industries boost economies and development, shows UN Report: Retrieved from http://www.unesco.org/new/en/media-services/in-focus-articles/creative-industries-boost-economies-and-development-shows-un-report/

[54] http://www.unesco.org/culture/pdf/creative-economy-report-2013.pdf

[55] Ibid, pp.156–159.

[56] www.youtube.com/watch?v=5lp4EbfPAtI

[57] http://portal.unesco.org/culture/en/ev.php-URL_ID=18668 &URL_DO=DO_TOPIC&URL_SECTION=201.html

[58] http://unctad.org/en/Docs/ditc20082cer_en.pdf

[59] http://www.tandfonline.com/doi/ abs/10.1080/10632921.1997.9942966#preview)

[60] https://www.gov.uk/government/news/creative-industries-worth-8million-an-hour-to-uk-economy

[61] P.13, http://unctad.org/en/Docs/ditc20082cer_en.pdf

[62] Ibid, p.14

[63] Ibid

[64] Ibid, p.15

[65] Howkins, John, *The Creative Economy: How People Make Money from Ideas,* London, Penguin Books, 2013.

[66] *A Study on Creativity Index,* Home Affairs Bureau and University of Hong Kong, 2005.

[67] http://en.unesco.org/creative-cities/home

[68] P.16, http://unctad.org/en/Docs/ditc20082cer_en.pdf

[69] Surat Al-Raad (Thunder), 17. Mufti Taqi Usmani translation via http://www.quranexplorer.com

## Afterword

[70] Alexandr Solzhenitsyn. Nobel Lecture, 1970 http://www. nobelprize.org/nobel_prizes/literature/laureates/1970/ solzhenitsyn-lecture.html